MW01254712

ALEEZA BEN SHALOM

GET MARRIED

Get *Over* Your Hurdles and *Under* the Chuppah

Marriage Minded Mentor LLC
362 B Montgomery Avenue
Merion Station, PA 19066
www.MarriageMindedMentor.com

Printed in the United States of America

First Edition

ISBN 148004590X
EAN 978-1480045903

Typesetting & Cover Design by: Joanna Brown

Editing by: Alisa Roberts

Dedicated to **Dr. Herb Caskey**, for your generous support over the years. You have been more than a good friend; you have been a pillar of strength for our family as well as the greater community. Your continued commitment to helping others is truly inspirational. This book is a result of that inspiration.

May you go from strength to strength.

This work is also dedicated in loving memory of
Shoshie Stern, Shoshana Rochel bas Elimelech, z"l.

May her memory be for a blessing.

Gratitude

To my loving husband, Gershon, my gratitude is eternal. Your support, patience and help with our family is immeasurable. I am complete because of you. It is because of our ten years together that I had the experience and insight to write this book. For all that you are and all you will be, I am loving you.

To my beloved children, Dovid Lev, Miriam Chaya, Moshe Chai and Yehuda Yosef, you are my treasures. I know that I have been on the computer a lot and you want to know what I have been doing. This book is the result of all those hard hours. However, my favorite hours are spent with you. You are most precious to me. May you grow and reach Torah, chuppah and maasim tovim.

Mom, you have been my greatest teacher. It's said that an apple doesn't fall far from the tree; I am proud to be the fruit of your labor. I hear your wisdom coming through in my words. You empower me to reach my potential. Thank you for encouraging me to follow my dreams, for believing in my ability to reach them and especially for guiding me on life's journey.

Dad, thank you for being the voice of reason. A dream is only a dream, but when it is practically implemented it becomes a reality. Thank you for helping me reach reality. Your mentoring and words of wisdom have guided me more than you know.

To my Mother-in-Law and Father-in-Law, thank you. You have loved me as if I were your own daughter. May all brides be blessed with this gift! A special thank you to my Mother-in-Law for her help with the book.

To Alisa Roberts, my editor and personal writing mentor, you have taught me more than any course in school. I have learned about myself, my style of writing and my abilities. Thank you for guiding me through this process from outline to final draft. Working so closely with you was a joy.

To Eric Ackland, the proud new owner of Amazing Books in Pittsburgh, you really are amazing! Thank you for your reorganization, editing and feedback on the rough draft. Your insight was eye-opening. May you be blessed with much success.

To my COO Melissa Keleti, you are a pleasure to work with. Thank you for all your work behind the scenes. I love your laugh, your positive attitude and I am grateful for your friendship.

To Joanna Brown, my cover designer, interior layout expert and friend, thank you for taking this project on and for working quickly to reach our deadline. A special thank you to my sister Jessica for her design ideas and expertise (she does invitations! www.asterstudio.net). Thank you Sarabeth for your savvy feedback and guidance on the book cover and Raizy for hours of proofreading.

To my relatives, mentors and dear friends, thank you for lovingly and patiently supporting me. Your mentorship and friendship are invaluable. Having good mentors and friends isn't just nice: it is essential to my success. I feel blessed to be surrounded by so many good people. I am afraid to name you individually for fear of leaving someone out. Just smile: you know who you are.

To all my clients, THANK YOU! Our relationships have taught me so much. You have each given me the opportunity and inspiration to do what I know best. May those who are single get married, those who are married have children and those who have children have grandchildren. And may you all merit to stay happily and healthfully married!

And to the One Above, thank You for all of my experiences. As my mother says, You provide "all good all the time." I understand that some of my greatest challenges have also led to my greatest rewards, for without the challenges I couldn't have become who I needed to be. And, of course, thank You for all the sweetness in my life. It keeps me going.

Table of Contents

Part IV: How Do I Know if This is The One?

Conclusion 127

Introduction

*T*his is not a book on how to date. You've probably read that one already. This is a book on how to get real and get married. Or, more specifically, how to get ready, get set up, get married and stay married forever. If this book has found its way to you, then I know you've been dreaming of meeting your spouse and having a family. I want you to know that I have the same dream for you, and I am writing and working for your success. *Get Real, Get Married* is a guide for self-actualization and success in dating for marriage... and beyond.

When I meet with prospective new clients, I specifically look for singles who are itching to be married. If that sounds familiar, you have picked the right book. If you are thinking about marriage but not sure, this book may help you to clarify your goals. If you are a parent, relative or friend of someone who is looking for their soulmate, use this book to help guide them (keeping in mind to also be good to them and support them with loads of love). I've included both personal growth action plans and success strategies for the marriage-minded. I offer tools to help you date consciously and put your best self forward. I teach you to understand yourself, prime you to be marriageable and help you to find satisfaction in the process.

How did I become the expert? That's a long story, but here's a piece of it. I always knew that I wanted to be a wife and a mother, but my career aspirations were hazy at best. As Lewis Carroll so cleverly put it, "If you don't know where you're going, any road will get you there." After graduating college I bounced around through a variety of education, volunteer and work paths but without finding my niche. This was when I began to ponder the meaning of life. What was my purpose and how was I going to achieve it? I had to be here for a reason. What was it?

I found my answer in traditional Jewish values. But that was only part of the answer; a general solution to a specific question. What was my part? At that point in my life I might not have known what I wanted to do, but I did know I really wanted a family. Yet I couldn't imagine it. And then, in the fall of 2001, I went to a friend's wedding.

During the dancing, my friend the bride got on the microphone and said, "Anybody who wants to get married, come get a rose and a blessing." (While giving blessings in general is very much a Jewish custom, this combination of flowers and blessings was just something my friend chose to do.) I remember sitting at my table, surrounded by the other singles, bewildered. It was the first time I had asked myself "Do I really want to be married now?" Right then and there I made the decision. I wanted to be married. I went up and got a rose and a new mission. My mission was to be engaged within a year. No more half-measures for me.

In May of 2002, eight months after I made that decision, I started dating the man who would become my husband. We got engaged a month later and married in October of 2002. Pretty crazy, right? If you're thinking, "Well, I picked the wrong person to take dating advice from. I don't want my life to look anything like hers," allow me to explain. I call myself thoughtfully impulsive. If I don't know what I want, I don't do anything; but when I know, watch out! I move mountains in a matter of moments. Who I am and how I do things in the world is not for you. It's my way, and I don't recommend it for anyone other than *me*. What I want you to do is find *your* way and achieve *your* life's purpose.

That is where this book comes in. I have spent a lifetime learning to understand myself and how I connect and relate to the world. I have built a successful business where I help others to rediscover themselves, and, in the process, find their soulmates. I began as a matchmaker, but developed into a mentor who empowers my clients. I am more than just a matchmaker or dating coach; as my now-married clients can tell you, I am a soul-tuner who will help you harmonize the signals you are sending out so that you attract your other half sooner rather than later. I have exerted enormous effort to make my hopes and dreams a reality. And now that my hopes and dreams have arrived, I'm ready to focus on yours!

This is where we get to the real work. There will be concepts and ideas presented, followed by action steps to get you going and solidify those ideas in your life. The right frame of mind is important, but it's the practical steps that will get you where you want to be. I recommend reading through the book once, then going back and doing the action steps week by week. Take the time to think through the ideas and don't skip the exercises. I know there's a temptation to assume that just thinking about your answers for a minute is enough. It isn't. If you want to see real change, you need to take real action. As it says in *Ethics of the Fathers*, "According to the effort is the reward." Reading is the first part of the effort; actually doing the action steps is the second part. It's like reading an article on healthy eating habits. You could just keep reading, but if you don't change your habits and you keep eating donuts every day then you won't see or feel the physical benefits of the information you've learned.

So grab a pen and let's get working!

Part I:
Are You Really Ready?

Chapter 1: Your Soulmate's Other Half

Look into a mirror. Take a deep breath and smile. You have now met your soulmate's other half. Did you catch that? Your soulmate's other half is YOU. You already have half of the puzzle in your hands. Unfortunately, the part of the puzzle we most often overlook is ourselves. Recognizing your other half is the second step to getting real and getting married. It's not always a popular idea, but you find the right person in the right time. Right now is the time to continue to become the right person. I want to help you learn to trust yourself, your intuition and the wisdom that the One Above gave you and continues to give you on a daily basis. The key to success begins with you. People often tell me that they think there is nothing they can do about their situation or that they have done everything they can and now they are waiting. But you can do something about your situation and "waiting" will not lead you to your other half. Though you have made real efforts in the past, you have a new opportunity now and an obligation to continue to grow. Trust me when I say that this growth is going to tip the scales in your favor and bring you one step closer to getting real and getting married.

Before we get started, I want to share one more thing. Jewish wisdom teaches us that forty days before a soul is conceived, a heavenly voice announces, "This woman and this man will marry." That means there is someone out there destined for you before you even were you. Although your spouse was created and designated for you, finding him or her is another task altogether. But keep in mind that 1+1=1. This is Jewish math; you and your spouse are two bodies that share one soul. We are not looking for perfect. Rather we are looking for ideal, for the person who is right just for you. You will love their good side and be able to manage their "other" side (more on this in Chapter 3). Your soulmate will help you to actualize your greatest potential in this world. They won't be perfect. What they will be is a perfect fit for you.

Chapter 2: All Beginnings Are Hard

We learn from Rashi, a famous Torah commentator, that "All beginnings are difficult." This is not a negative thought; it is a Universal principle that Judaism teaches us. And I think it is important that you are aware of this principle right from the start so that when things are difficult you can understand that this is normal and not become discouraged. For example, have you ever skipped the beginning of a book, opened up to a random page and started reading from there just because? Do you sometimes read magazines backwards, flipping from the back to the front? Why do you do this? I believe it is because you intuitively or instinctively know that "All beginnings are difficult."

How can you motivate yourself to get started when you know it will be a challenge? If you don't understand that beginnings are difficult, you may end up going from enthusiastic to disillusioned, which eventually leads to giving up. Instead, let's prepare your mind, heart and soul for the journey you are about to embark on. If you expect challenges when you start something new, you won't be discouraged when you face them. Know that challenges are a part of the process. It's supposed to be this way.

If you think you are at the beginning and you don't see any challenges, maybe it's not really the beginning. And if you have been dating for the past ten years and don't think you are at the beginning, think again! You are now trying a new approach to dating, which means this is another beginning, and I expect that it will come with some difficulty. I am not saying this to discourage you. If you have not found your soulmate yet and have been searching, even for a long time, I believe that you are close to the end of your journey.

Here's one last little secret to keep you going. While all beginnings are difficult, the difficulty is often brief. Things will become easier over time. Yes, really, it will get easier.

Action Plan

Make a list of things that were hard for you at first but that you found became easier over time. Take time to reflect, internalize and accept that all beginnings are hard.

Chapter 3: Thoughts and Attitudes: Good vs. Other

Thoughts have power. The thoughts that run through your mind are what lead to the things you say, which in turn bring about your actions. This means that what you think will impact every aspect of your life. *That* you think is not within your control. Thinking is from the One Above. But what you choose to hold on to is within your power.

Be conscious of your thoughts. There's a gift in this consciousness: when you tap into your awareness you can choose to let go of a thought you have been holding on to and allow space for a new thought to enter your mind. This technique takes daily work and a recognition of what's happening moment to moment in your mind. But it's worth the effort; being present in the moment will benefit you in all areas of your life.

Now that we've discussed thoughts, let's talk about attitudes. Because who wants to date someone with a bad attitude? Have you ever been out on a date with someone who is bitter, angry or depressed? Not so much fun. Dating can be a pleasant experience even when the person you're dating isn't the one for you. The key to that is in your attitude.

Have you ever heard the phrase *good vs. bad*? I want to introduce you to my revision of this phrase. I call it *good vs. other*. The first aspect of attitude to examine is how you approach life. For a moment, I want you to focus on how you see the world. I'm not asking whether you see the glass as half empty or half full; I want to know whether you even see the glass. And if you see it, what do you call it? Your attitude – your disposition, approach, feeling and state of mind – is affected both by what you see in the world and the way you express what you are seeing.

Have you ever made a list of the *good* and the *bad* in a relationship? Have you ever tried to weigh both sides so you would know how to proceed? It gets a bit confusing, right? Let's add some clarity to that list before you even start weighing sides. I want to start by re-titling your categories. In every relationship there are at least two sides of the picture. The traits, qualities and characteristics that you like and value are filed under *good*. For example, if your date is ready and waiting for you when you come to pick her up, you may notice that she is considerate. Or if your date holds the door open for you, you might notice that he is kind. Many of us value the traits of consideration and kindness and would list these traits under *good*.

Now what about the other side? Can you recall a time when you listed all the complaints you had about a special someone? When the *other* was weighed in with the *good*, the scales didn't always tip in favor of continuing the relationship. But still you felt conflicted. Your decision to continue or break up was still a toss-up. Why is that? It's because the *other* is not a list of bad traits. Rather, it is a list of those things that you don't prefer. For example, what happens when someone runs late or forgets to hold the door open? Thoughts start to race. "She doesn't respect me and my time," you might think. Or, "He doesn't value me." But what really happened? What actually happened was probably that she has a bad habit of running late. Or that he was careless this time and forgot about the door.

Other is not the same as bad. *Other* things are simply those qualities that you don't prefer. So here is the bottom line, the question you really have to answer: if this trait clearly falls under *other, will I choose to live with it?* What I mean by live with it is: can I patiently wait for my spouse to possibly change, or even patiently wait a lifetime and not let it drive me crazy and pull us apart? If the answer is, "No, I don't want to patiently wait it out or never see a change," then this trait is not an *other* trait, it is actually a deal-breaker for you. And a deal-breaker breaks the deal, period.

It is hard to imagine living with something that you know will bother you day in and day out, right? Right! I hear you. Think for a moment about your family members. I'm sure there are things that bother you about them. I'm sure there are things that bother you about roommates, friends and co-workers too. It's just the way of the world. Because you are not identical to any other person, there will be things that bother you about others. If you have a high tolerance for difference, you will find it easier to be around people in general. If you have a low tolerance for difference, you can expect others to bother you more often. Figure yourself out. Marriage will be easier or harder for you depending on your tolerance threshold. For now, don't try to change or judge yourself. Instead, identify who you are and accept it.

Action Plan

Pick one time throughout the day to recognize what's going through your head. Understand what thoughts you're holding on to. Acknowledge those thoughts and set them aside for the moment. See what else comes to mind.

Make a list of things that bother you about a loved one. Figure out and write down how you've managed to live peacefully with those traits that you don't prefer.

Think about a time when you had a friend or acquaintance with a trait you couldn't handle, and describe for yourself how and why you steered clear of that person.

Chapter 4: Laws of Attraction

Continuing on the theme of thought, remember, the thoughts that enter your mind are from the One Above; however, the thoughts you choose to hold on to are in your hands. The Law of Attraction, a philosophical idea dating back to the early 20th century, states that like attracts like. Whether your thoughts are good or bad, positive or negative – whatever you focus on is what you will draw to yourself.

There are two approaches to this law that can help you improve your dating experience: you can change your approach to the negative, and you can open your mind to the positive. Let's begin with the negative.

Do you feel like you always get the negative, boring or weird dates? I'm not saying you are any of those things. (*Are you?*) Seriously though, what are you? Why are you attracting those individuals into your life? Evaluate yourself. What are the things that you are focusing on and projecting out into the world? Taking the time to really examine your patterns will empower you to make a change from within.

Now on to the positive! You've heard of the placebo effect. This is a great example of attracting positivity. We know from countless medical studies that when a person believes that a medication will help them, even if the medication turns out to be only a sugar pill, they will fare better than those who don't believe. Let's apply this knowledge to dating. When you believe that you will be getting engaged in a year, even if that thought is not based on anything solid, is it possible that you will fare better than those who don't believe? Yes! Based on this principle, it's likely that you will. Your belief in your ability to achieve engagement and marriage is a fundamental part of the process. You've probably already noticed that my belief in your ability to get real and get married is positive and strong. What's your belief? Still need a sugar pill? Go buy a candy. You can enjoy the sweetness knowing that the cure is in your thoughts!

But there is one more aspect of this law to keep in mind. Ever heard of the nocebo effect? The nocebo effect is the opposite of the placebo effect. If you take a medicine believing that not only will it not work, but that it will do you harm, you can injure yourself physically, mentally and emotionally just from the thought. It is still only a sugar pill. But because your thoughts were different, so was the end result.

Notice your thinking. Are you more positive or more negative about dates, dating and the opposite gender in general? Are you neutral? Negative thoughts can harm you and positive thoughts can help you. Neutral thoughts don't count toward the positive, and they are not as benign as they seem. Anything other than positivity is negative when you are trying to accomplish your goal of getting real and getting married.

Stretch beyond your limits, expand your mind. Slowly transform your thoughts and draw your soulmate closer to you one thought at a time.

Action Plan

Sit down and examine your thoughts. Are you more positive or negative? What are you drawing to you that you want to change? What are you drawing to you that you want to increase?

Pick one thing you can focus on that will draw what you want to you. Take note of what changes over the next few weeks.

Start a positive list of your favorite aspects of dating and the opposite gender. If you find yourself thinking negatively about either, add another item to the list.

Chapter 5: Develop an Attitude of Gratitude

Now that you've identified your emotional state and understand the importance of thought and attitude, the next step is to work on some practical tools for developing and improving your attitude. These steps will change your physical, mental and emotional tune.

You know that voice in your head that sometimes convinces you to do something you know is wrong? "Don't even bother; what's the point? You're never going to get married, " it tells you. That negative, but oh-so-convincing, voice that pounces on your hopes and dreams and tells you that you're silly for even believing in them? That voice's greatest resource is depression and sadness, two things that don't look pretty on anyone ever (let alone on a date). After months or years of dating, one is more susceptible to this voice. But now you're going to work on crushing it. The following exercise will help you develop an attitude of gratitude, chasing away any negative or defeatist feelings. You can start to live happily ever after... right now! And as I discussed in Chapter 4, as if you need more incentive, positive feelings and energy have a way of attracting soulmates.

Take out a piece of paper, a journal or your favorite electronic device.

Think about all the reasons you are grateful that you were given this time to be single. You may need to take a deep breath, close your eyes and dig deep to see some of the gifts that the One Above has provided for you. The goal is to leave any bitter, sad or angry feelings aside and to focus on gratitude.

At the top of your page write: "I am grateful for being single because..." Now it's time to get writing. Keep writing until you can't come up with anything else. If your list is less than 20 items, please close your eyes again and dig deeper. Your list should include 35–100 things you are grateful for. If I asked you for a list of your top 100 complaints about being single, I am sure you could write it with ease. So I have total faith you can write about gratitude too!

Carry this list with you every day for one week. Read it a minimum of once in the morning and once in the evening. On top of this, add at least one item to the list per day (adding more would be even better).

If you start to feel down, sad, sorry for yourself or hopeless during the day, take out the list, read it and then add a minimum of five things you are feeling grateful for. When you can't list anything else about your gratitude for being single, then start on generic gratitude. For example, you can be grateful for the ability to think, sing or see. You can be grateful for the sun or the rain. If you are really stuck and can't come up with anything to add, stop, take a minute and remember that there is always another way of looking at things. You have the ability to shift your thoughts and to allow yourself new ways of thinking. Also, keep in mind that gratitude doesn't have to be deep to be real. Simple gratitude for your most basic functions and needs is a great place to start.

Here's a sample list which you can use as inspiration should you get stuck.

- I got to travel to Colorado, Boston, Philly and Israel more times than I can count.

- I get to live on my own.

- I know that I can do anything I want to.

- I had time to get a master's.

- I know how to cook.

- I had time to learn to play piano.

- I know how to add oil to my car.

- I know how to advocate for myself.

- I can stay in the shower as long as I like.

- I can spend a whole evening on self-development without neglecting anyone.

- I learned what my taste in music really is.

- I made all sorts of friendships that I wouldn't have made otherwise.

- I can walk out the door at a moment's notice.

- In theory, I can go on a road trip to Maine with only a backpack.

- I can take three bags without anyone kvetching about my luggage.

- I can talk on the phone for an hour uninterrupted. I can do this repeatedly in a single night.

- My money is both mine to earn and mine to spend.

- I can go to evening classes or the gym after work.

- I can always go to my parents when I want to.

- No mother-in-law!

- I eat according my tastes without having to accommodate someone else.

- I have a one-gender kitchen.

Set yourself up for success. I want you to be mentally, physically and emotionally healthy. Expressing gratitude will help you to gain perspective. When you are thankful for what you already have, you will be less likely to focus on what you don't have and instead be grateful for all the new things that come your way.

Action Plan

Compile a gratitude list.

Read it twice daily.

Add one or more things to your list daily.

Make gratitude your attitude!

Chapter 6: The ASK

So what do you want? Do you know? If you do, give yourself some credit because you're already ahead of many people. (And if you don't know, don't worry! The action steps over the next several chapters will help those who don't know to figure it out and those who do to clarify further.) But it's not enough to know what you want. You also have to ask for it. Like a child who has to ask a parent for all their wants and needs, you too must ask for what your heart desires. We'll start with the basic Ask and get more specific as we go.

I want to be engaged and married. The thing you are generically asking for is to be married. So be honest: do you want to be married? Really? Are you willing to put this desire front and center? Yes or no? If no, put the book down and pick it back up when the answer is yes.

Still holding the book? Great! You want to be married. Your desire to be married now is probably stronger than it has ever been. You can't imagine waiting another year or two or three or five or ten... are you feeling anxious yet? Good. We're on the same page. You want to take steps towards getting real and getting married. So ask for it. Really ask for it. Through your words, your tears and your actions, ask. There is One Infinite Source and Power in the world that can answer your prayers. I can't. I have a job to do here, but I don't run the world. You can't. You have your own job, and you don't run the world either. So the only thing you can do is pour your heart out and ask for what you want.

Now let's get in to the specifics. What are you doing? Asking for what you want. Who are you asking? The One Above. How are you going to ask? You are going to be specific. Perhaps you've heard the Rolling Stones song "You Can't Always Get What You Want." If not, here's the chorus:

You can't always get what you want
You can't always get what you want
You can't always get what you want
But if you try sometimes, you just might find
You get what you need

There's a lesson here, even if it wasn't the one Mick Jagger intended. Notice that the line *"You can't always get what you want"* is repeated three times. Not once, not twice – three times. *"But if you try"* – if you are specific, if you ask for what you want, if you are clear about who you are, well, *"You just might find you get what you need."*

OK, you get it: be specific. But I'm not just asking you to think about being specific. I'm asking you to take a little practical step in order to bring the message home. I want you to write a letter asking for what you want. There's a sample letter below if you want some help getting started.

Lastly, this letter is not the end of the asking process. You can't write a letter once and forget about it. You should continue to ask for what you want every day and revise your letter about once every other month. Over the course of time you may notice that what you ask for will change. That's OK too! Ask today for what you believe you want and need today, and ask again tomorrow for what you want then. The basic rule is just to keep asking the One for everything you want. You don't have to say it in the perfect way, just as long as you ask.

Here is the sample letter. You can write your own or you can elaborate on this one. You can add your personal preferences and what you are specifically looking for. You may or may not get what you ask for but that doesn't, and shouldn't, stop you from asking.

To the One who runs the world,

I want to be engaged, and I want to be married. Please help me. I want to date those people who are appropriate to be my spouse. I don't want to suffer through this process. Help me accept what You give me. I want others to stop asking when I am getting married and what's wrong with me. I want to build a future with my spouse. I want to live, love, learn and grow. I want to feel happy and complete. I can't do it on my own. I need this other person in my life to take me to the next level. Please send him/her. I eagerly await my wedding day. Please grant me clarity and a good support network.

Your patient and persistent,

Bride-to-be/Groom-to-be _____

Now it's your turn. Here are some suggestions for beginning your letter:

I want...
I don't want...
I need...
Please help me...
I can't...
I feel...
I hope...

Action Plan

Take the time to gain clarity on what you really want.
Write a letter asking for your specific wants and needs.
Continue daily to ask the One to give you what you need.
Review your letter once a month and revise if necessary.

Chapter 7: Push What? Pushka

Pushka. It's Yiddish for charity box. What's the connection between your Ask and charity? Consider the following analogy from Rabbi Avrohom Chaim Feuer in his book *The Tzedakah Treasury*:

"The relationship of tzedakah [charity] to prayer [the Ask] is comparable to the relationship between seasoning and food. Just as spices and seasonings bring out the real flavor locked inside the food, so does charity bring out the tremendous power locked up inside words of prayer. Therefore, it is most effective to give some money to charity before praying."

You don't have to be religious to ask the One Above for something. When are you most likely to reach out and ask spontaneously? Most likely you hope, ask and pray for something when you are desperate to get what you want. Whether it's health, money or a husband or wife, when you really want it, you know how to ask for what you want. But it's important to recognize that there is an additional component to asking: giving. They go hand in hand. If marriage is something you want, then you should pursue it with all your heart, all your soul and all your resources. So your practical step for this week is to set aside money for charity every day. Choose a charity or fund to donate to, designate a certain amount each day and make your contribution after one week. It is important to develop the habit of giving once every day with intention because soon you will be giving to another for the rest of your life.

Action Plan

Begin each day by setting aside money for charity. Do this either with a note or physical bills. (At the end of the week you can tally the total and send a check.)
Share what you are doing this week with someone close to you. If you want to, invite them to join you in giving charity as there is power in numbers.
In the merit of finding your soulmate, choose a fund that supports a needy bride and groom.
Donate the money after one week.

Chapter 8: "Green" Speech – Words Matter

Pulling money from our pockets is much easier than pulling the right words out at the right time. To accomplish this, it's important that we are able first to listen to the words that come out of our mouths as well as paying attention to how others speak.

We all know that words matter. This concept is even clearer during the dating process. What someone said or didn't say, or even how they said it, can determine the outcome of a date. The intentions behind our words can make or break relationships. And what we intend to say is only half the battle; the actual words we say matter even more. We all have those phrases and words in our vocabulary that we know we need to clean up. Maybe it's something you've been thinking about. Or perhaps a friend pointed out a word or phrase you often use that is doing you more harm than good. Take some time to think about what's on your speaking to-do list. Make a commitment to pay attention to your words for one week. Pledge to guard your speech. We are often careful and picky about what goes into our mouths. Let's be equally careful about what comes out.

Rabbi Michael Stern created the 10 Habits of "Green" Speech and the pledge at the end of this chapter. Before we get to that, let me tell you a little about Rabbi Mike. He is one of my mentors. He officiated at our wedding and has been guiding us ever since with marriage advice and Jewish wisdom. He is known as the Rabbi Without Walls and one of the programs that he created focuses on going verbally green, or, as he calls it, "Green" Speech – The Ethical Principles of Speech. He explains it this way: "We have begun to go "Green" in taking ethical responsibility to rid our environment of the toxins, pollutants and carbon footprints and have adopted an eco-filter as to the food we eat, products we buy, cars we drive so let's extend those ideals to the words we say and take responsibility to adopt "Green" to our speech. We must get rid of the poisonous and toxic words that often come out of our mouths and the vocal imprints we often leave on one another. We won't accomplish this overnight but the first step is to try."

Whether dating or just in everyday life, the 10 Habits of "Green" Speech will be a guide for you to achieve success in all areas. Focus on one habit each day for 10 days. In general, you are likely to be more pleasant, attractive and likeable after you adopt these behaviors. Common sense tells us to behave this way but daily life proves that it is sometimes easier to be sarcastic and critical. Try these habits on for size and see how your dating life improves. You have nothing to lose but your negative attitude!

10 Habits of "Green" Speech

1. Make only positive statements and refrain from making derogatory ones – even if they're true.

2. Promote people's well-being. Don't make any statement that could cause someone physical, financial or emotional harm.

3. Humor is great, but make sure jokes aren't at someone else's expense.

4. Avoid speaking badly – even about yourself.

5. Communicating derogatory or harmful statements by writing, verbal hints, or body language is just as bad as saying them.

6. It takes two to gossip. Don't listen. Change the topic or walk away if necessary.

7. Give others the benefit of the doubt.

8. Refrain from conveying negative stereotypes or information about a group of people or organization.

9. Communicate with your spouse [or the person you're dating] and family with kind and supportive words.

10. Warn a person about potential harm; for example – from a prospective business or marriage partner. But make sure your information is accurate.

"Green" Speech – Words Matter Pledge

Please take a minute to think about each of the following principles:

- I will try to take ethical responsibility for the words that I use and speak "Green."

- I will try to see how negative, harmful and derogatory words and gossip hurt people, including myself.

- I will try to replace hurtful words with words that are positive, healing and encouraging.

- I will try to choose words that make people feel accepted, empowered, respected and loved.

- I will try to use words that cultivate harmony, peace and unity in our homes, schools and organizations by choosing words that foster cooperation, teamwork and productivity.

Signature:_____

Action Plan

Sign the "Green" Speech – Words Matter Pledge.

Read the "Green" Speech – Words Matter Pledge once daily.

Reflect about your day. Journal your successes and your challenges (list a minimum of one success or challenge each day).

Chapter 9: The Quickest Way to Get Married: STOP DATING

This is one of my favorite phrases. Does it bother you? Before you skip this part, give me a chance to finish my thought. I think you'll see where I'm coming from.

The shortest distance between two points is a straight line. But what if there are things blocking that nice straight path? You can try to hike your way around them and risk getting lost in the process, or you can take the time to clear the path before you start walking down it. Often the quickest path to marriage is to stop dating and organize your health, living situation, job and personal life.

...and Start Dating Yourself

I know you know yourself, and I also know that you are always changing. It's always valuable to look in the mirror to see if who you think you are is aligned with who you actually are today. Often when I tap into the present moment and take the time to think, I realize that I have an outdated view of myself. That view of me can be as old as yesterday, last year or last decade. Take time to be alone with yourself and work on yourself. It is important to consistently do self-evaluations and check in daily, weekly or at least monthly to see who you are becoming.

What if you feel like you haven't changed? That too is an important piece of information. Consistency in actions and behaviors may be an indicator that you are being held back by fear. Then again, it could mean something else altogether. You won't know what it means until you give yourself some time to think about you. How do you go about checking in with yourself? Try asking the following questions:

Who am I today and how am I different from who I was last month?

How does this current way of being benefit me?

Do I feel a need to change any character traits or my direction in life?

Am I feeling grounded right now, today, in this moment?

What new goals do I want to set for the next 30 days?

...and Get Your Health in Order

From doctors' appointments to dental surgery, we all have things that come up from time to time. I am talking about all those little appointments and things on your to-do list that are getting in the way of looking, feeling and being your best.

And what about the major things, like going on a diet, committing to a workout program, seeing a therapist or changing your drinking or smoking habits? If you feel that you have a major health issue that you want and need to get in order, prioritize your schedule and get it taken care of. I know this is not as simple as I make it sound. Some of my clients join gyms, attend Overeaters Anonymous meetings, get personal trainers or see therapists weekly. These things are not simple for them either, but it's an important part of the process.

Here are a few clarifying questions to help you figure out what health issues are a priority.

How has your health changed in the last 3 years?

Are there any appointments you've been avoiding or putting off? Why?

Are finances holding you back from taking care of your health?

What do others nag you about that you also feel is important?

Who do you trust to help advise you or support you in achieving your health goals?

List 5 health items to get in order over the next 6 months to a year.

When you feel confident that your health is in order you exude an energy that is attractive to others. Which is why it is often important to place your health goals above dating for a period of time. How long? That depends on your goal and your circumstances. I wish I could tell you exactly how long you need, but you will have to determine that with your mentor. When you get your health in order, from the inside out, you will feel more confident when dating.

...and Move to a New City, State or Country

If you are thinking about making a move in the next three to four months, here's some advice: don't date through the transition. Make the move and then date. Or maybe you don't need to move at all. When you are planning a move, or even thinking about the idea of moving, you go from a physically and emotionally stable place to a place of instability. From the moment you have a strong urge to make a change you become distracted.

Let's speak for a moment about the idea of not moving. What about the idea of putting your big move on hold? Is your move imminent? Think about whether it's really necessary. You may want to move out and live on your own. Or maybe you want to get out of your apartment and buy a house. Stop for a minute and think about your situation. What if you tabled the idea of moving for three months? Could you handle that? Is that a reasonable request? As I mentioned above, the moment you start to focus on moving you remove your focus from dating. If you don't mind putting dating on hold or on the back burner, then moving may be an option. But if you are marriage-minded and do not want to delay your engagement and marriage, consider waiting to move unless absolutely necessary.

A client of mine used to live in a home that had all sorts of problems. Mold, no heat, bug infestation... the list goes on. This is an example of someone who needed to move. He made the move immediately. However, because of the stress of the move, he was then sick for several weeks. It delayed the soulmate search for about two months, and even then things weren't 100% back to normal. Even a necessary move is likely to cause major upheaval in your life. Moving, along with starting a new job and getting married, is among the top three stressors in life. So think about your desire to move, evaluate and act accordingly.

On this note, I had a client who told me that she wanted to move out of her parents' home. Everything there was fine; she just needed a change. She thought a move would do the trick. I suggested tabling the idea for three months if the move wasn't an emergency. After three months, if nothing was happening in the dating world, she could reconsider moving. She agreed that the idea of the move was consuming and distracting her. So she held off. Within a month she started dating someone seriously. As you may have guessed, they got married, and she did move... in with her husband, not out on her own!

But what if you are marriage-minded and you want to make a big move, what should you do? You want to get married already! The thought of not dating for even a week makes your skin crawl. What if I told you that you could meet your soulmate faster if you did not date through the move? What if you were happier, healthier and more balanced because you did not date through transition? I know this concept is going to be hard for some of you to swallow, so here's a story to encourage you to rethink your moving and dating strategy. Rosie* and I spoke years ago. She was ready to be married. She was balanced physically, mentally, spiritually and emotionally. So what was the problem? She was planning to move overseas in two months. She wanted to take one last look and try to find her husband before she left the U.S. So I asked her a question. "Imagine you meet your husband in the U.S. in the next two months. Would you be willing to give up

---

* All names have been changed to protect the privacy of those involved.

your big move? Would you be OK with living in the States instead of overseas?" After a little thought she told me, "No." Rosie felt strongly about moving, and she did not want to stay even for the prospect of meeting her soulmate. "But maybe he will come with me," she said. I told her, "This is my personal opinion, but I believe if you do not want to live here, then you need to focus your energy, make this move and say your good-byes. Your soulmate will be waiting for your overseas." How does the story end? Rosie stopped dating, enjoyed her last few months in the U.S. with a clear head and a peaceful heart. She moved overseas and started a language immersion class. On the first day of class she met a man in the hallway. Today, three years and two kids later, they are happily married. When I reminded her of this recently, she told me that not only had she gone to class that day not thinking about or expecting to find someone to date, but her future husband was actually taking a break from dating. She added that she thought this helped both of them to just be themselves – leading to a very happy ending. I can't tell you that all endings will be as sweet as this one, but what I can tell you is that the quickest way to get married is to STOP DATING... and take care of yourself and your needs.

Action Plan

What is on your plate right now other than dating and getting married?

Clear your plate – accomplish your list.

Stop dating and take care of yourself and your needs.

Chapter 10: Blood, Sweat and Tears

I'm not going to sugarcoat it: sometimes blood, sweat and tears are necessary to get from here to soulmate. Allow me to explain.

Blood

In the world of Jewish dating, it is known that Tay-Sachs disease is a Jewish genetic disorder. Many of you may know to get tested to see if you are a carrier. What you may not know is that Tay-Sachs is not the only gene to be concerned about. There is actually a whole list of Jewish genetic diseases. Both Ashkenazi and Sephardi Jews have their own lists. And what if you aren't genetically Jewish – should you still get tested? Great question.

As with all Jewish genetic diseases, Tay-Sachs is only an issue when both partners are carriers. If one side of the couple is a carrier and the other is not, then there is no concern. If you are not genetically Jewish, it is less likely that you would be a carrier for a Jewish genetic disease, but screening is often still recommended.

Dor Yeshorim is a great support to those in the Jewish community. They conduct anonymous genetic screenings before engagement which help to reduce the number of children born with a genetic disease. Other options include going to your local doctor and asking where to get screened or contacting the Victor Center for the Prevention of Jewish Genetic Diseases. Knowing if you are genetically compatible will save you heartache in the future. It is worth the small amount of blood that you have to give to get the information you need.

So what's the bottom line? Research what all of this means. I have certainly not given you enough information to make an informed decision. I have merely brought this subject to your attention so you can investigate and make a decision on how you want to proceed. Please not that this is primarily an issue for those of you in the childbearing years.

Sweat

Dating should be enjoyable and pleasant. However, just like a good workout, you should sweat a bit to get the best results. What do I mean by sweat a bit? If you are in the honeymoon phase of the relationship, where everything is so great and you can't imagine ever not liking or not getting along with the other person, then I suggest you get suited up for a workout. The honeymoon phase lasts only so long. And you need to see all sides of your soulmate. A good workout will let you see how your intended handles stress. When the body begins to be taxed, it sweats to cool itself. It is a self-regulating mechanism that preserves the body and helps it to maintain optimal health.

Sweating happens during both physical and emotional times of stress. But everyone handles emotional stress differently. Some people sweat more, some less; some maintain their cool temper while others heat up and become argumentative. It is important for you to know how you handle stress and how your soulmate handles stress.

Sweating is a healthy activity. While you should not nudge just to nudge and create a problem where there isn't any, you can certainly watch for your potential soulmate's reaction to stressful situations. Is this a person you can envision staying married to forever? Be confident in moving ahead, or be clear about your concerns.

Tears

Searching for your soulmate is an emotionally demanding process. As you move through it, you will probably have moments of frustration and sadness. You might feel like sitting down and crying. Maybe you should! Crying doesn't have to be a negative thing; it can be helpful.

Tears are a valuable part of the process. It's easy to get caught up in the sadness and miss the value of the tears. But tears don't have to only be about sadness or frustration. They can also be an outlet for relief, a validation of your own feelings and a deeply-felt prayer. In fact, there is a long history of using tears in prayer.

Did you ever wonder why the Western Wall is also referred to as the Wailing Wall? It is because of all the tears that have been shed there over the centuries. It has been our tradition to whisper our prayers at the wall, to stuff our notes in its cracks and to leave our tears. But you don't have to jump on the first plane to Israel to deposit your tears at the wall. Wherever you are, your tears will be, and have been, collected and accounted for.

Not only are your tears collected by the One Above, those tears are also heard by your soul. Your inner yearnings and deepest desires are validated by your tears. You will most likely feel a sense of relief when you finally sit down and have a good cry. Can you remember the last time you did this? How did you feel after? Did you feel a sense of relief? Were you quiet and calm after the experience?

If you haven't had a good cry in a while you might want to think about opening up to it. If you cry almost every day you might want to think about how you can have a healthy release without overwhelming yourself. No matter which end of the spectrum you're on, coming to the middle ground will help you feel more balanced.

Action Plan

Do your research about genetic testing and decide how you want to proceed. If testing is what you want to do, make the appointment.

Keep an eye on stressful situations. Learn how the one you're dating handles stress so that you can avoid potential problems.

Evaluate where you are on the crying spectrum. Make sure you are feeling balanced and that you value the tears you shed.

Chapter 11: Take Your Emotional Temperature

Take your emotional temperature right now. What does it read? Are you happy, sad, confused, hopeful, relaxed, anxious? What's going on inside of you today? I am not looking for you to change this state of being, just to acknowledge it. Accept it. Record it and take your temperature daily or (if that is too much to handle) weekly. I want you to see clearly in your own life that, as King Solomon so wisely put it, "This too shall pass." After taking your emotional temperature for several weeks, you will start to see that you aren't always getting the same reading. Some days you will be up, other days you will be down. This is normal and healthy as long as the emotional swing isn't too wide. An extreme emotion, whether positive or negative, will throw you off balance. One of my goals is to help you to maintain stable and balanced emotional levels. Your first step is to identify the state you are in. Only then will you be able to attempt to make a change. Keeping in mind this lesson of King Solomon, you are more likely to see the larger picture and not get stuck in any moment or emotional state.

Action Plan

Today my emotional temperature reads _____

Make a list or chart of positive and negative states. Take note of your trends.

Decide what you need to work on in changing your emotional state. Make an effort this week to shift your temperature so that you feel more grounded and balanced.

Part II:
Know Yourself

Chapter 12: What's the Problem? You're Looking at It!

"I think you're looking at it." Those terse words were spoken by Joseph J. Hazelwood, captain of the oil tanker Exxon Valdez. He was responding to U.S. Coast Guard officials who questioned him after the vessel under his command ran aground in Prince William Sound in March of 1989, resulting in a massive oil spill. In the end, Captain Joe pled the fifth so as not to dig himself into a deeper hole. But what did he really mean? Was the mess the problem? Or was it that he, the captain responsible for the vessel, was the problem?

Don't we really all have that problem? The mess is often easy to see, but understanding who is responsible for it can be much more difficult. We tend to blame others when we really should be accepting the responsibility ourselves. But it's important to realize that taking responsibility empowers us to own up to our thoughts and actions and make changes where necessary. Choosing how to live our lives is in our own hands. By realizing this, we can direct ourselves onto any path we choose.

The first thing to understand about yourself is whether you are dating-minded or marriage-minded. Are you a serial dater who enjoys (or who doesn't enjoy but just can't stop) dating? Have you ever met a person who kvetches that they want to be married, who goes out over and over again, but who never has success? Either everyone is not for them or the ones they want don't want them. How about someone who is either driven by physical infatuation or is an experience junkie without a purpose? Or those who think they want to be married, but when it comes down to it find that living with another human being for the rest of their lives involves too much compromise? Toilet seat up, toilet seat down, dirty clothes everywhere, neat freaks... who needs it? I assume most of you can't relate to this. If you want to be married, be prepared to make changes. If you like yourself the way you are and aren't prepared to accommodate change, then stop pretending you are dating for marriage. Or at least please tell the rest of the world you are just dating and not dating for marriage. Should you change your mind, you can then change your status.

Since you are reading this book, I'm assuming you are marriage-minded. Committing to being marriage-minded isn't your problem: so what is? What is standing in the way of you getting what you want? It's time for us to go deeper within to find the answers.

Chapter 13: Mission Statement: Your WHYpower

Why do you want to be married? Notice that I'm not asking you if you want to be married. I'm asking WHY? I know you want to be married; I know you have the willpower. But when your willpower isn't enough to get you married, it's time to combine your willpower with your WHYpower. What is your WHYpower? It's clearly understanding your core values and using them to help you achieve what you want in the short and long term.

Write below a list of reasons that explain why you want to be married. Don't make judgments about your reasons. Don't even think about them for too long; just write the first thoughts that come to your mind. Keep writing until you've run out of reasons (you may need extra paper).

_____

_____

_____

_____

_____

_____

_____

Is this a question you've already considered? I hope so. Knowing why you want to be married is the foundation for getting engaged, getting married and staying married to the same person forever. I imagine your list above probably includes some selfless reasons, maybe some selfish reasons, some universal human reasons and perhaps some Jewish reasons. Whatever is on the list, it is not for judging but rather for noticing why you want to be married. Here are some example reasons from my clients:

I want to get real and get married because...

> *I want a connection.*
>
> *I want to be a wife/husband and mother/father.*
>
> *I want to share life with someone.*
>
> *I feel incomplete.*
>
> *I want a commitment.*
>
> *I want to give.*
>
> *I don't want to be alone.*
>
> *It's a mitzvah (commandment).*
>
> *I want to reach my potential.*

Imagine you are happily married, because you will be soon. Now, of course, even the happiest couples fight, right? When my husband and I were engaged, we received what I affectionately called the "Icky Marriage Book." Actually, we received two copies! Page after painful page spoke about conflicts that married couples have and how they resolve them. I closed the book and put it on the shelf, saving it for some guest who might enjoy reading such depressing things. The second copy we re-gifted to people we thought might need it more than we did. Little did I know that soon the "Icky Marriage Book" would lay open on our dining room table for weeks as I eagerly devoured page after necessary page.

After two months of being married, we hit a low point. Out of frustration and desperation to get my husband's attention, I declared, "Marriage is too hard. No one told me how hard this was going to be. I think we should cut our losses and get out before we have kids." Can you say OUCH! I thank the One Above every day that my husband was wise enough to reply, "I don't know what's wrong, and I don't know when or how we're going to solve it, but we have a lifetime to figure it out. So whether it's today, tomorrow, next week, whenever, we'll figure it out." Being married for over a decade, I can tell you that my WHY has kept me going when my will wasn't enough. While I regret ever having said that, I learned a valuable lesson from the experience: living by your WHY while working through challenges is not only the best way to get real and get married – it's also the best way to stay happily married.

Action Plan

Live by your WHY. Make a note or put a reminder on your phone that pops up daily to remind you of WHY you want to be married. Complete this sentence:

I want to get real and get married because...

_____

_____

_____

Chapter 14: What Makes You You-nique?

What makes you YOU? What differentiates you from the thousands of other singles out there? I ask all my clients this question, and more often than not they say, "What do you mean?" Here's what I mean. There are hundreds of thousands of people in the world looking for their soulmates. With the invention of the internet, the world has become much smaller and at the same time has expanded your options a thousandfold. So how are you going to promote yourself and explain to the world who you are and how you differ from every other man or woman out there? Sometimes describing those differences, even though you see them clearly, can be a challenge. What you say to describe yourself may make sense to you but not to someone else. So not only do you need to be clear for you, you also need to be skilled in your delivery of yourself to others.

When you make it known to others that you are available, they will inevitably ask you, "So tell me about yourself." What are you going to say? Will it differentiate you from the thousands of other men or women out there? Start to name the things about yourself that are less common. Or the traits that you have to an above-average degree. Some examples from my clients:

I am someone who...

lives life as if the glass is half full.

is passionate about giving to others.

smiles often.

appreciates worldly things.

understands people.

is calm and has a calming effect on others.

is in tune with my surroundings and other people's thoughts and feelings.

does secret acts of kindness.

is loyal and devoted.

has a zest for life.

is quiet yet competent.

has the ability to get along with anyone.

Now make your unique list of what you are looking for in your soulmate.

I'm looking for someone who...

has an engaging personality.

is sweet but has an edge.

knows how to both give and receive.

is not critical.

is handy.

is wise beyond their years.

is powerful without raising their voice.

is comfortable in the silent moments.

has made life decisions I can respect.

can be my rock and ground me.

Are any of the things listed above very unique? No, but everyone is a unique combination of the traits that make us who we are. That is a level of unique too. Start thinking outside of the box. Make a long list of what you think makes you special. Don't spend too much time thinking about it. Just start writing.

Action Plan

Write out a list of different traits that describe you. Include traits that are unique and even those that aren't; you may find something unique in the combination.

Compile another list, this one describing what you are looking for.

Narrow down your lists so that you have an articulate, one- or two-sentence answer to the question, "So nu, what are you looking for?"

Memorize these sentences and practice saying them so that you sound natural.

Chapter 15:
Are You Different From Who You Were a Year Ago?

In what ways are you different from who you were a year ago and how do these changes benefit you? Good question, right?

All too often you don't see your own growth. It is easy to see growth in someone who was single, gets married and has a child. It is easy to see how their life has changed. But if you've been single for the last several years, or for a decade or two, you may be less likely to recognize your own growth. And it may be even harder to see how that growth has changed you for the good. That's right, I said it: being single has changed you in good ways.

It is easy for a thirty-something single to look back and say the opposite. "Years ago, I was more idealistic, flexible and easygoing. Now I'm older, bitter and desperate to be married." However, when my clients dig deep they usually come up with ways in which they've grown. They have done things they couldn't have done if they were married. They have had time and space that wouldn't have been available to them with a spouse and children. You may be frustrated that you aren't at the next stage of life, but let's not forget to recognize the good in your current situation. This can help you build on your attitude of gratitude, which in turn will help you put your most appealing foot forward.

Action Plan

I am different _____

_____.

This benefits me because _____

_____.

Chapter 16: Your Bucket List

What's left to do before you meet your soulmate? Do you have a to-do list? Travel the world, lose weight, get a job, get a degree, get a higher degree... the list goes on. At some point in our lives we all have a to-do list. How long or short is that list right now? What is still left on your list? How are you going to go about accomplishing those things – what action steps will you take to achieve your goals? Plan your timeline. Yes, I actually want you to write out the list, your timeline and your action plan. (Come on, you're good at this by now!) Is anything on that list getting in the way of you meeting the right one? If so, can you accomplish that goal more quickly, within the next two months? No? Then perhaps you can reevaluate and see if you can eliminate it from your list. Maybe you don't really need it on your list at all.

The goal of evaluating this list is so that we dot the i's and cross the t's. If you tell me you want to get real and get married, I believe you. But if you say you want to get real and get married this year and then you tell me that you are traveling every other weekend, starting a new job, moving to a new city or taking night courses four nights a week, I am likely to tell you that you are standing in your own way. It is important that you clear a path. Make yourself physically, mentally, emotionally and spiritually available. Because someone is going to come along and take up your physical, mental, emotional and spiritual energy, time and space.

And what if you have nothing left on your bucket list; what if you've crossed everything off? That's a good place to be. Now, just add one more item, "Get real and get married!"

Action Plan

Write down your bucket list.

Evaluate your list and decide when each item will be accomplished or if it can be crossed off your list.

Start accomplishing your list ASAP.

Chapter 17: A Compass and a Watch

"Where is my tardy lost husband? I'd like to buy him a compass and a watch!"

One of my clients once said this to me. Could it be true? Could your soulmate be lost? No, he's not late and he's not lost, but buying him a watch is actually a Jewish custom. Yes, I'm serious. Look it up.

So you think your husband or wife is lost? They must be if they haven't found you by now, right? You are so busy looking for your soulmate that you forget to continue to look for yourself. Forget about buying him or her a compass and a watch and check your internal compass instead. What is it reading? Do you think you are headed in the right direction? People are often busy watching the clock and saying "Where is my soulmate? Where is my soulmate? Where is my soulmate!" They become trapped in the waiting. This world is not designed for waiting. There is something for you to do during this time. What are you supposed to be doing besides waiting?

As for a watch, keep an eye on your own time. Do you think time is flying or moving too slowly? How are you passing your time? Are you using time wisely? This is your time and your time is now. Let's break out your compass and watch and use them to direct us closer to the core of you. Keep an eye on how much time you are spending on yourself. At a minimum, you should have twenty minutes to evaluate your positioning on a daily basis. Keeping a record of how much time you do or don't spend on yourself will help you to know if you are really working on yourself or only thinking about it.

Now that you have designated time for yourself, what are

you going to work on? Perhaps your relationships with friends and family, your work or business growth or your personal health goals. You are not avoiding the search for the right person; on the contrary, maintaining your search is key to your success. But don't spend hours upon hours in any one area. Split your time reasonably between looking for your tardy lost soulmate and following your inner compass toward your own personal life goals.

Why do I want you to make an effort in this area? You will be a happier and healthier person. Which means you will be exuding a more attractive energy. A male peacock fans his feathers to attract his mate. In what ways are you fanning your feathers to attract your mate? Remember that your soulmate is also looking for you. You will be much easier to spot if you embrace your positive attributes and express them regularly to the world.

Action Plan

Reclaim the compass and the watch: stop wondering where he or she is and start keeping track of yourself.

Spend twenty minutes daily evaluating your personal goals and accomplishments. Decide how you would like to spend your time, apart from waiting.

Maintain your search for your soulmate in a balanced way. Don't let it take up so much of your life that you become depressed and lost in the process.

Remember that this process will help you to become more attractive to your soulmate.

Chapter 18: Engaged In a Year

Anything can happen in life. Man plans and G-d laughs. Actually, I tend to think it's more likely that G-d plans and man laughs. (Or at least I like to laugh; it's a better option than crying.) Either way, you have the best intentions of being engaged in a year, so for now we are going to believe it is true. Positive reinforcement and positive affirmations can retrain your brain and manifest a statement into your reality. So keep affirming!

Do affirmations make you feel more relaxed, happy and positive? Wonderful! But what if they don't resonate? There could be several reasons you aren't connecting to the idea of affirmations. First, positive affirmations may be new to you. New isn't bad, it's just different and unfamiliar. Give yourself some time to become comfortable with positive affirmations. Another reason you may not connect is if you don't feel connected to this timeframe. If being engaged in a year is not your idea or vision, then recalculating your timeframe may help you to become at ease with the affirmations. Lastly, there are reasons why even people who do want to get engaged in a year don't become engaged within that timeframe. Besides the obvious reason that the One didn't deem it to be your time, sometimes people who are more complex or have a more complex life situation (i.e., divorce, children, health issues or past trauma) may require more time to reach engagement. Having said that, I know many people who have complex life situations who still reached their goal in a year or less. This is not to discourage you from trying to move things along in a timely fashion. Rather, it is to alert you that you may want or need to pay more attention to your situation and exert a more focused effort to reach your goal. I believe positive affirmations are a great tool to help you focus in a meaningful and productive way on reaching that goal.

Regardless of your situation, your thinking is what will move you forward. Positive affirmations will have a direct effect on your thinking. To fully understand affirmations you need to keep three people in mind: who you are, who you were and who you are becoming. Who you are is only who you are in this very moment; this image isn't static. Who you were isn't who you are now; it is a past image of yourself. Who you are becoming is up to you; it is not yet your reality. Positive reinforcement and affirmations will help you meet challenges and smoothly transition from who you are to who you are becoming.

I affirm that you are going to live a vibrant, happy life with your soulmate. I know you are making good decisions that will make your journey easy and short. You are pursuing your dreams at the right time and with the right intention. I envision you smiling on your wedding day. Your journey is one of joy.

Here are a few affirmations for you to say:

I will pursue my dream of marriage and achieve my goal.

There is no distance that is too far for me to travel to make my dream of engagement and marriage a reality. I have the ability to connect my thoughts with my actions and to make good decisions that will bring me closer to my soulmate. I open my heart in a healthy way to those I date.

The longest distance in the world is between your head and your heart. This is not to discourage you but to bring to your consciousness the inner challenge you will face on your journey. Knowing what lies ahead of you will help you to prepare for the adventure. So grab the right tools and transform your dream into a reality.

I have a clear understanding of who I am and what I want.

As I look in the mirror at my body and soul, I reflect on who I am today. I accept and love all parts of myself. I trust if there is something that needs to change, I will notice it and take action. I love growing and continuing to become who I am meant to be. I am free to choose a soulmate who best suits who I am and supports who I want to be.

Knowing yourself today is great. However, when you look in the mirror tomorrow you may notice the image has changed for both the inner you and the outer you. Learn to do daily evaluations so your self-image is current.

I have a plan and also accept The Plan.

I have a plan, and I work on my plan daily. I accept with gratitude what happens to me as part of the Divine Plan. I appreciate all that has come my way. I smile often at others and receive smiles in return.

Your job is to make a plan of action so you can reach your goal. Yet at the same time there is a plan that is divinely inspired for you. Be conscious of both as you make your way to marriage. Smiling through the process will not only make your time more enjoyable, it will also help you to be most attractive to your mate.

Action Plan

Think about what else you would like to affirm and write your own affirmation.

Read your affirmation aloud daily for one week.

Part III: Get Ready, Get Set Up, Get Married!

Chapter 19: Matchmakers and Mentors

Why choose a matchmaker when you can do it on your own? Get with the times! Not only are there matchmaking dating sites, there are even popular matchmaking shows on TV! Matchmaking is the way of the modern world. And matchmaking isn't just new and in, it is old and traditional too. *"Matchmaker, matchmaker, make me a match, find me a find, catch me a catch!"* Remember that song? It's not just *Fiddler on the Roof* that teaches us that using a go-between, a matchmaker, is a healthy way of finding a spouse; Jewish tradition happens to agree. If you want to just date, you don't need a matchmaker. But if you want to find your spouse – the person you want to marry, live with, perhaps have children with and grow old with – then I suggest you consider using a matchmaker.

To explain this a bit further I'll share what a mentor of mine taught me. There are three types of matchmakers. The matchmaker In Fact, In Act and Intact.

The matchmaker In Fact is the one that says, "You and you should go out." Anyone can do this job. From the very young to the very old, we all have the ability to put people together. I'm not saying that the match will be a good one, but one doesn't need specific credentials to be the matchmaker In Fact. And you very well might find the best matches come from the most unexpected people.

The matchmaker In Act is what I refer to as a mentor. As Robert Kiyosaki articulated so well in his book, *The Cashflow Quadrant*, "A mentor is someone who has already done what you want to do... and is successful at doing it. Do not find an adviser. An adviser is someone who tells you how to do it, but has not personally done it." I value having a mentor for any area in which I wish to achieve success. If I want to change a habit, eat right, exercise or lose weight, then I want to partner with a like-minded person to mentor me and help me reach my goals. I have greater success in a shorter amount of time when I have a mentor partnering with me through the process. Not only does a mentor empower me to succeed and to accomplish all I need to in this world, but he or she is also able to bring me down from a high and up from a low. Remember our lesson from King Solomon, "This too shall pass." This phrase refers both to the good things and to the other things that happen in the course of a lifetime: the highs will fade and the lows will improve. A good mentor will shed light on your situation and help you maintain that balance. A mentor is a gift, another set of eyes and ears, a different understanding and perspective. She or he will keep you focused and accountable and help you to reach your goal of getting real and getting married.

The matchmaker Intact, who is also your mentor, is the one who helps you when the relationship with your potential spouse hits a low. Sometimes in dating you may want to walk away from a relationship when you really needed to pursue it, or vice versa. Your matchmaker Intact will help you hold things together. In short, they will help you get over your hurdles and under the chuppah.

Here is an interesting piece of matchmaker trivia: one is obligated to pay their matchmaker. Matchmaker's gelt (money) is divided into thirds between the matchmaker In Fact, In Act and Intact. Sometimes the person who made the match In Fact also helped you In Act and Intact. In that case, they receive the full financial payment. Often though, someone will make your match In Fact, but another person will be your support In Act and Intact. In this case, the person In Fact is paid 1/3 and the other person is paid 2/3. You get the idea. How much does one pay their matchmaker? A matchmaker will sometimes make their fee known. If there is no specific fee requested, find out the local customs.

Now that we understand matchmakers let's speak more about mentors. In *Ethics of the Fathers*, we learn that one must have a good friend. Where can you find such a person? Who is qualified to be a good friend and act as a marriage-minded mentor? Great questions. There are several things to look for when choosing a mentor. A marriage mentor can be someone you know or someone new in your life. You don't need a long-standing relationship with someone in order for them to be your mentor. You also don't have to hire someone to do the job. However, it is within reason to hire someone so that you can have the support that you want when you need it most, without feeling guilty that you are bothering someone.

A marriage-minded mentor will be:

Healthfully married for 5+ years.

Someone you can trust and confide in.

Someone with wisdom (in other words, a history of making good decisions and giving good advice).

Someone who is available to speak for a minimum of 45 minutes weekly, uninterrupted. (Uninterrupted means no call waiting, no kids screaming in the background, no work intruding. You are the priority for that block of time.)

The key is to find someone who is invested in you. That means they know you or are invested in getting to know you. Why? Because you have the answers for you. You know who you are, and you know who you need to be. You already know what you need to know to be successful. The only thing you may not know is the fact that you already know. A mentor is there to help bring out what is within you and provide you with perspective. If you're serious about getting married, solo is not always the fastest way to get there.

Investing in Yourself

You are exactly who you need to be in this moment, although you may want to remodel a bit too. This is not a contradiction. The remodeling doesn't take away from your current state of perfection; you're simply investing in yourself. But don't do it by yourself. You need a community, a team of experts to support you. What is the mentor recipe for success? Take one hand, extending your fingers with your palm open towards you. You are in the middle of your palm. Each finger represents one mentor. Your thumb represents your main mentor.

Caution: Too many cooks might spoil the broth. Which is why you need to limit the number of people you are speaking to and working with. Some people prefer to keep their personal life private. For those in this category, you need only one mentor to work with and count on. Others might think I'm crazy for saying you need to limit yourself to a maximum of five mentors. Between family, best friend, Rabbi or community leader, old friend, new friend and the hairdresser, you may already have over ten mentors or people you go to for advice. Aleeza's rule for success: minimum of one and maximum of five mentors. If that's really a stretch, you can count both parents as one – because they really are one soul, just in two bodies!

When working together with your mentors, it's crucial that everyone shares one goal: your success. This relationship is about you, not them. Your success will likely come from a quiet, intuitive place inside you. My clients often think they must ask others for advice; or rather, sometimes think they can't trust themselves. However, trusting yourself and your gift of intuition is one of the best things you can do. Having the right mentors to guide you on the journey will not only increase your likelihood of success, it will hopefully make your whole process more pleasant.

Know Yourself, Share With Others

Once you've set yourself up with your mentors, let's make sure that you're giving them the most accurate and up-to-date information. Be sure to share, simply and clearly, who you are and what you are looking for. Let's clarify for a minute because I don't want you to get stuck on "Who am I today and what am

I looking for right now?" I know we've discussed this before, and I'm mentioning it again for two reasons: it is vitally important, and it's a challenge that I face over and over again with my clients. When I speak about who you are, I am asking who you are right now in this moment. I want you to share with others who you are now. Why wouldn't you do that? Sometimes you may share who you were, not who you are. Other times you may share who you aspire to be which is also not who you are. In order to gain perspective, I suggest you make three separate lists: *Who I was, Who I am* and *Who I aspire to be*. In addition you can also list *Who I was looking for, Who I am looking for* and *Who I hope my spouse will become*.

After you've made these lists, review them. Is this what you think? Or is this what someone else has told you? I've had hour-long conversations with clients about this topic, and in the last ten minutes a client will tell me, "Oh, what I told you isn't what I think; it is what my _____ (mother, friend, neighbor) says about me or thinks I should be looking for." We then have to spend even more time going back and redoing the exercise so we both know what my client thinks instead of what others are telling them to think. I want you to know yourself. For this exercise, don't ask others what they say about you or about what you want or need. Go within and decide for yourself.

I thank the One Above daily that I married someone who was on target with my then-present self, who lined up with who I used to be and who was headed in a similar direction. Even with all of that in balance, there is still daily work. But it is a huge blessing that we have our history in common, our present in sync and our future visions aligned.

Once you have your lists, you will be more ready to answer the infamous "So what are you looking for?" Once you've answered the question, be ready for off-the-cuff suggestions. When a friend, relative or amateur matchmaker makes an off-the-cuff suggestion, here is the correct response: "Hmm, sounds interesting. What makes you think we would be a good match?" Ask for specifics. "You mentioned that she's sweet and kind. Can you tell me what else you know about her?" If you get a generic answer like, "I don't know, don't you trust me?" – you do not have to say yes just because you don't want to hurt them. Say no. Why? Because you are hurting yourself, and perhaps another, more by going out on a date that is not appropriate. People like to play matchmaker. Some do it well. Others just put men and women together based on the fact that they are the only two singles they know, even if they don't know you well enough to buy you a sandwich let alone set you up with your spouse.

Please don't misunderstand me. There are many friends, relatives and neighbors who have made great matches. I am not speaking about those intuitive individuals. I am speaking about the people in your life who just want to see you happy and will say or do anything to try to make it happen, even if it's not logical. I am giving you permission to politely say "no, thank you" when you are confident a match isn't for you.

Chapter 20: What is Your D.E.W. Date?

What's a D.E.W. date? Allow me to explain. Pretend that for today you run the world. Anything you say not only comes true but the One Above agrees with you. Got it? Good. So let's make a timeline. When would you like to start dating? Supposing you meet your soulmate on that date, when would you like to get engaged? And after that milestone, how long would you like it to be before you are standing under the chuppah?

D_____ E_____ W_____
(Start to Date)   (Engagement)   (Wedding)

I've asked this question to many singles, and everyone has a different answer. Some tell me, "I want to be dating yesterday! Should I meet my soulmate right away, I want to be engaged in about three months and married four months after that." Others say, "I need to finish grad school. I'll be ready to date in three months. If I met my soulmate immediately, I would want to be engaged after eight months and married a year later."

There is no right or wrong answer to this question; there is only your answer. But we need dates! Remember, I asked you to imagine that you ran the world for a day, which means you are free and clear to dream away. Why is this a key component in the process? There are sometimes things that are already scheduled in your life that won't allow you to achieve your goal. For example, if you say, "Sure, I'd love to be engaged tomorrow and married next week!" I would answer, "Really? That won't really work for you because you probably want friends and family members at the wedding, and you will need to give everyone enough notice." So it's not a realistic goal; it's an unrealistic comment that doesn't align with your hopes, dreams or reality. What if you want to get engaged in two months and married four months after that and then you look at your calendar and realize you booked a trip that you aren't willing to cancel? That's why you have to get real to get married. Look at your real life, your real schedule and what is happening today and in the coming months. See if your plan aligns with your life. Now you're ready to plug in dates. Let's say that today, as you read this, it's January 1st. With the first plan in place (three months to engagement, four months to marriage), you would start dating today and meet your soulmate today, January 1st. Engagement after three months puts us in April which then leads us to an August wedding. Make sure to include the year when you fill in your own dates. (This is only a sample plan, not yours. Don't panic!)

D_____ E_____ W_____
(January 1st, '14)   (April 1st, '14)   (August 1st, '14)

Does that sound right? Feel right? Does it make sense with all that you have going on in your life? Maybe yes, maybe no. If you look at your estimated D.E.W. date and it doesn't look right, sound right or feel right, reevaluate. You will know when you have it right because you will look at the timing and think, "Yup, I can D.E.W. that. That will work with my life, family and schedule."

Chapter 21: K.I.S.S.

Sorry if I enticed you into reading this chapter because of its title. I hope you're not disappointed that we aren't actually speaking about a kiss. (If you can't wait to read about the physical aspects of relationships, see Chapter 30.)

So what are we speaking about? K.I.S.S. – Keep It Simple, Silly. What do I mean? Sometimes we're so smart, we're silly. In the modern world we are all so advanced. Our technology, our lives, our education – everything moves at a rapid pace. If you don't get into the best schools, get that degree, then an advanced degree, you start to feel as if you are lacking. And if you think you need those titles and accolades, then you probably think your spouse must match up.

When looking for a wife, my husband was given some good advice. "Men and women are different enough. Find someone you have something in common with." Wise words. But in terms of education, it's not so easy to find commonalities these days. The more advanced degrees we pursue, the further we differentiate ourselves from each other. We create unnecessary divisions. Don't misunderstand me: I am not saying that the education you worked so hard for is unworthy. It certainly is worthy! But it's important for you to understand how to integrate and align your education with your dating expectations. When degrees start to define who you are willing to date, you may lose out on good opportunities for marriage.

Some women want a man who is well-educated and advanced in his career. Other women may not be as particular but still want, as we all do, someone they can respect. And for many women respect is tied to education, which in her mind may directly impact his ability to earn a living.

On the other hand, a man may or may not want a woman who has a degree and can earn a good living. Many do; after all, second incomes are the norm today. But if she earns more than he does, or has letters other than Mrs. before her name, it may make him feel inadequate. He might think, "She doesn't need me, she can support herself." And men, in many cases – you are right! The modern woman can get along without a man. She can work, earn a living and even raise children all on her own.

However, and here's the point, both women and men need a

close relationship with one another. Without that ,we lack the connection and oneness that comes from uniting two bodies and unifying their souls. This unity comes from the two becoming one. No one can accomplish that on their own.

So how do we overcome the great education divide and bring some clarity to modern decisions on what makes a good spouse? K.I.S.S. Keep It Simple, Silly – your educational expectations, that is. Yes, as my husband's mentor said, we do need to find someone with whom we have a lot in common. However, perhaps we need to reevaluate our educational expectations. Am I asking you to lower your standards? No. Keep every standard you have of marrying a quality person. But think about lowering your expectations. Your expectations are only preferences. As a dating mentor, my preference is that you align your desires with your reality and base your commonalities on things such as positive character traits, direction in life, religious orientation and common future goals. Before you decide if your date went to the right university, maybe you want to see if the insides match the outsides. Keep It Simple, Silly, and leave your BAs, MAs and PhDs hanging on the wall where they belong. After all, they're for business purposes, not for marriage credentials.

Chapter 22: 10 or Fewer 'Til Spouse

I want to bring consciousness to your dating. I want you to be cautious when choosing whom to date. Imagine for a moment that you are getting engaged in a year... because you are. What if I told you that you only get to choose a maximum of 10 people to date (one at a time, not all at once!) before you get married.

Play this game with me for a minute. Ten or fewer. You're going to be a little choosier, aren't you?

Can I guarantee that if you follow my advice you'll meet your soulmate in under ten setups? No. Because I do not run the world. Am I going to yell at you if you get to ten and haven't picked a spouse? Of course not! Ten or fewer is the number of people I hope you will date before you get engaged. You don't control the time of your engagement and neither do I. But from here on out you can change your thoughts and your actions in order to help yourself reach your goals. If you want to meet a challenge, you set a goal for yourself so that you have something to reach for. Why should dating for marriage be any different? By having a number in mind you have a built-in countdown to keep you motivated, as well as permission to say no to any match that you already know isn't a good idea for you. This is no guarantee. However, it is an easier and healthier way of dating for marriage.

Think of it this way. Even if you do everything for your health— eating right, avoiding stress, exercising – you still have no guarantee that you will live to see 120. But you do know that, statistically speaking, you have a much greater opportunity for health and well-being in both the long and short haul if you do make good health choices. In my experience with my clients, following these action steps will lead you to a happier and healthier life. Not everyone gets engaged in a year, but you are still obligated to do your part. So what is your part?

The mental process of thinking in terms of ten or fewer should help you to prioritize who is most likely to be a match. You don't have time to waste when dating for marriage. You can do as you please, but if you are looking to get real and get married then prioritizing is a must. First, eliminate those potential dates that shouldn't be on your list at all. You know which ones. The ones you have a gut instinct about. Listen to that instinct; trust your gut! You don't have time for pity dates or guilt-trip dates. Just because someone makes a suggestion doesn't mean that you have to go out. Politely ask for more information. If you don't have enough information to make a decision, delay agreeing to a date. And if you still don't have enough and they keep bugging you – "He's a handsome doctor, and he's Jewish too!" "She's pretty, sweet, kind, I really think you'll like her!" – don't be fooled into thinking that someone else knows you better than you know yourself. You have the greatest insight into yourself. Get enough information to make a proper decision. Don't be afraid to choose carefully and don't feel guilty about your choices. These are your dates and no one else's.

"But Aleeza, the whole world is open to me! How can I close myself off to so much?" I agree, the whole world is open to you. That's actually a big problem! The only limitations you have are self-imposed and if you don't impose any restrictions, you can't filter what you are viewing. Choosing ten or fewer will help filter your options, which in turn will not only give you direction but encourage clarity as well.

How do you pick those ten? Let's evaluate. First, I want you to identify any patterns that you notice in your dating history. What type of person have you dated? Do you date similar types of people or totally different types of people? Do you find people you are dating to be ready for marriage or still figuring themselves out? Do you have a certain physical "look" that works for you, or certain "looks" that don't work for you? What similarities and differences do your previous suitors or ladies have in common?

Take a few minutes to compose a list. This list is a tool for you to gain clarity on how to proceed in the future. Let's say that you notice from your list that you have dated all different types of people; you don't have one type, you don't have one look. What does this mean? It could mean that you don't know yourself well enough and are trying different people on for size. This will eventually help you get to know yourself better, but it will be at the expense of dating people that are not in the ballpark. This type of dating hurts both you and them. As someone once told me, if this isn't your wife or husband, she or he belongs to someone else. Proceed with caution.

Let's look at this from a different angle. What if you date all types of people because you are so varied and find things of value in all people? So you don't have a type; sometimes it works better than other times, but really you could see yourself with a number of different types of people. You are just not particularly fussy. This type of dating is fine. Singles who are less fussy sometimes have to wait for the other person to say yes to a first date, as they are more inclined to say yes more easily. How can you attract your mate? Perhaps you can be a little more choosy – not about personality or looks, but about how strongly your prospective date desires to be married. If you are marriage-minded and plan to get real and get married, then choosing someone of like mind is a high priority. Be fussy about finding a marriage-minded, datable single.

Consider this analogy. Say I have a pair of glasses, and I lose them in my house. I look all over for the missing glasses, but I can't find them. How will I search for them? In the beginning I'll search often and with purpose. But after about a week my vigor will wane. I'll start to give up. When will I search for them? During the parts of the day when the room is brightest. Say that doesn't work either. What if I then remember that sometimes the best way to find something is in the dark with a flashlight? Because the whole room is dark, I won't be too distracted by other visual stimuli. I can only see what my flashlight illuminates. Everything else in the room is outside of my attention as I focus on one small area at a time. Should I not find what I'm looking for, I'll shine my light elsewhere. And if I see my glasses in the dark I won't just gloss over them; they will stand out. In short, I'll likely find my missing glasses sooner and with greater ease. How do you do this when looking for your soulmate? Think in terms of ten or fewer.

Chapter 23: Where to Meet the Right One

Sometimes clients ask me, "Where can I go to meet someone? What is the best place?" That's a great question, and I can't answer it! Where are you most likely to meet your soulmate? Where are you least likely to meet? Only you know the answers. Do you think you will meet at a singles event or weekend retreat? How about a holiday table, or maybe through a friend or relative? There's the online option too. When I ask my clients, "Where are you most likely to meet your soulmate?" I usually hear strong opinions and preferences. "Oh, I can't stand online dating; I've had enough bad dates." Or, "I need to meet someone as a friend first, or casually at a dinner table or event."

Your preference, whatever it is, isn't right or wrong. It's your preference. I like starting with your preferences, with what makes you most comfortable. If you aren't having any success with your preferred method after a few months, you can move on to other options. As you know, all beginnings are difficult, so it doesn't make sense to increase the challenge and go against your preferences. We'll start inside your comfort zone; there will be plenty of time to move outside of it later! Start with what you know and like. You like dating online because you are more reserved and don't make a good in-person first impression? Great, start online. You don't like dating online because you are a social butterfly and this method leaves you without your wings? Skip online dating for now and head to some singles gatherings where you'll be more comfortable. And remember, I asked for your preferences and not for anyone else's preferences. For this step, I don't want you to ask other people where they think you are most likely to meet someone. Save their opinions for another time. I can't tell you how many times my clients have answered the question, "Where are you most likely to be comfortable meeting someone?" with someone else's opinion. Everyone thinks they know what is best for you. In reality, I believe you know where you are most likely to succeed, and I want to hear from you!

If you have tried your preferred method of dating and it's not working, then it's time to reevaluate and try one of your less-preferred methods or a suggestion from a friend. Know your preferences and try them first. If at first you don't succeed, try what you don't prefer!

I prefer to meet someone_____.

I am less likely to meet someone_____.

Chapter 24: Pick One

That's right! Pick one person to date. I'm asking you to choose *whom* you date in addition to being the chosen one. Because you are now clear about who you are and what you are looking for, I am empowering you to pick the next person you are going to go out with. If you are someone who doesn't get a lot of potential matches, it will be harder for you to say no even if someone doesn't sound right. In addition, saying no can be especially challenging if you have had a long break since your last date. However, I would much prefer you date one person every three months and have those dates be good dates. Rather than the alternative: dating several times a month and building up a long list of experiences you wish you never had. On the other hand, if you have a list of five or more "options," I want you to pick who you go out with next. This is not just a line where first come is first served. You are choosing who is most likely to be your spouse, not only who was first suggested and available.

I once had a client who had two potential dates to choose from. The first person who contacted her about her future Mr. Right didn't have his dating profile and couldn't answer specific questions. My client received only generic information about this *amazing* guy that she *had* to meet. Mr. Right #2 was suggested to her with full details and a written profile including a photo. Dilemma: what do you do when you are closer with the person suggesting Mr. Right #1 but you lack info? Ask for more info. Which is just what she did. After several days without any new information, I suggested she choose Mr. Right #2 to date for now. Not only did we have information, but what we learned about him really lined up with her. I also reasoned that should *it* not work out, hopefully her matchmaker for Mr. Right #1 would have more info by the time she moved on from #2. But we'll never know more about #1 because she married Mr. Right #2!

Pick One also means that you pick one person and to the rest of the world you are unavailable. Unavailable really means unavailable. Don't bother even thinking about any other suggestion. If anyone calls to tell you about this great person you must meet, simply let them know you are not available right now but that you'll let them know if that changes (and don't give them any more information unless they are one of your five go-to people). Listening to a suggestion will only distract you. There's no way for it to benefit you – you don't have the freedom or the attention to pursue it and it will impair your vision in your current situation. When you wear glasses in the rain, they fog up. When it's "raining" men, or women, your vision gets foggy too.

But what happens if you accidentally say yes to two people who both get back to you at the same time? You just went on two first dates: now what? A client of mine got stuck in exactly that position and called me in a panic! After we spoke, she decided it was only fair to give Mr. Right #1 a real chance. She was honest with Mr. Right #2, apologizing and telling him that she would follow up with him should this not work out. After one more date with #1, she had clarity and called it off. Right away she called Mr. Right #2 and said, "Please take me out again." He completely understood, readily agreed (yes, he's amazing) and took her out. I recently received an email from her announcing their engagement! She thanked me for the Pick One advice and was glad she had handled herself and her dates with respect and care. Being considerate of your time is important, but it's even more important to be considerate of others.

Pick One additionally refers to picking one major thing to focus on in your life. As I mentioned earlier, the top three stressors in a person's life are moving, job change and marriage. When it comes to dating for marriage, our goal is stability in all areas of your life. We are about to rock your single status, and we need to be prepared for the shift that is about to occur. So please pick one thing to focus on. If dating is not a #1 priority, then don't date. Wait until you can make it #1. I hear some of you saying, "What if it is never #1?" Well, your spouse will appreciate you making them #1 even before their arrival. So don't be afraid to own up to your dreams and put your future spouse first now.

"But Aleeza, I'm in grad school, and I really need to keep up my GPA." If you are going to grad school, fine, go. Just know that dating is your #1 priority. So if you have to skip a class for a date or get a B instead of an A, that's OK. (You can try bringing this book in as an excuse note, but I don't think it's likely to work.) Be prepared to suffer the consequences of putting dating first. You may not graduate with a 4.0. But then again, you may not care if you are walking down the aisle before graduation.

Are there exceptions to picking one? Yes and we'll get to that in House Rules (Chapter 33).

Chapter 25: Three Dates in Ten Days

You've picked your one. Now we're on to how to go through the dating process with what I like to call technical success. Technical success is going from date to date in a reasonable amount of time without wasting time between dates or wondering where this is going.

What do the first two weeks of dating typically look like for you? Do you talk on the phone, getting to know each other before meeting in person? Do you have a phone call and a date? Do you go out twice in that span, maybe once per weekend? Well, I'm putting you on the accelerated schedule. From the time you both agree to a date, I want the two of you to fit three dates into the next ten days. Yes, three in-person dates in less than two weeks. Of course, if you don't like someone after the first or second date and you have clarity, by all means move on! Three Dates in Ten Days is a concept that is geared for gaining clarity.

This advice is most helpful if you both live locally. However, what happens when you are dating someone out of town? The ideal is to follow this advice but to modify it and understand that some dates may be back-to-back. For example, if someone comes to town on a Sunday, you have date number one. Then the following weekend one of you travels, and you have back-to-back dates Saturday night and Sunday day. It may sound like a bit much, but after the second weekend, I am confident that you should have enough information to make a decision. If you continue dating, you have clarity; and if you decide to move on, you can do so with confidence.

There is also super-long-distance dating where someone comes in for a few days or a week at a time. This may require three back-to-back dates or every-other-day dates. I imagine you're starting to get the hang of how to handle Three Dates in Ten Days.

I know this concept may be outside of your comfort zone. You might be thinking, *"Aleeza, I have a life too, I don't just date for a living!"* As you know, all beginnings are difficult. Because we know that beginnings are difficult, we need to give your new relationship the best opportunity for success by opening it with some momentum. We need to get things in motion before your head starts to swim. Otherwise you risk a phenomenon I call Make-Believe Relationship. Make-Believe Relationship happens when there is too much time between dates. Your mind is excited about the new relationship, so it focuses on it. But since not much is going on, it starts filling in the blanks with imaginary, and often wrong, information. Sometimes this means self-sabotage: you convince yourself that the other person isn't interested. Other times it means setting yourself up for disappointment: you make up stories of how amazing things are going after only one date. But there is a simple solution to getting out of your head and on to actual dates. Clear your schedule, set a date and give your mind something real to focus on.

Is there another option besides Three Dates in Ten Days? Yes, and I think you may be able to relate to the following scenario. You go out on a Sunday. Then, because you are both so busy, you wait until the following Sunday. The same thing happens the following week. Now you're going on three weeks and you've only seen each other three times. If you have good feelings about the potential relationship, the wind has been taken out of your sails. If you have neutral feelings about the relationship, your head has had three weeks to invent problems, which you start to believe because you don't have enough information to make a proper decision. If you have negative feelings about this relationship, you are now mad at yourself for spending almost a month dating someone you could have known was wrong for you from the beginning. Unfortunately this is sometimes the only option you have and you should do your best to keep the momentum going. When possible, it's best to incorporate Three Dates in Ten Days to achieve greatest success.

Chapter 26: The Laws of Dating E-Motion

Keeping things in motion will provide you the momentum to know whether your date is leading to chuppah or back to your doorstep. This is why I've developed the laws of dating e-motion.

What's so great about momentum? Well, if we're already exploring this, I figure why not go to the expert? I present to you the laws of dating e-motion, based, of course, on Newton's laws of motion.

Newton's First Law of Motion

"An object in motion tends to stay in motion. Every object in a state of uniform motion tends to remain in that state of motion unless an external force is applied to it."

Aleeza's First Law of Dating E-Motion

A feeling in motion tends to stay in motion. Every feeling in a state of uniform motion tends to remain in that state of motion unless an external force is applied to it.

This law of dating e-motion applies equally to positive, neutral or negative feelings. Therefore, if on a first date your feelings are positive, those positive feelings will continue as long as the relationship continues unless an external force – such as too much time passing between dates, gossipy friends or bad behavior on future dates – is applied to it.

If on a first date your feelings are neutral, those feelings will continue as long as the relationship continues unless an external force – such as too much time passing between dates, greater enjoyment on future dates or a deeper connection – is applied to it.

If on a first date your feelings are negative, those feelings will continue as long as the relationship continues unless an external force – such as a miracle – is applied to it.

When there is a lag time between the first, second and third dates, the lack of follow-up allows the force of time to act upon your feelings. This is when doubtful thoughts creep in and your feelings can change. However, if there is a first date and a follow-up within 48 hours (either a call or another date), then the continued progress gets the dating process in motion and positive e-motions are able to stay in motion. Neutral e-motions can be analyzed and resolved more quickly and negative e-motions can be confirmed.

Newton's Second Law of Motion

"An object with a certain velocity maintains that velocity unless a force acts on the object to cause an acceleration."

Aleeza's Second Law of Dating E-Motion

A relationship with a certain velocity maintains that velocity unless a force acts on the relationship to cause an acceleration.

A couple with a certain velocity can maintain that velocity. However, if you are dating for marriage, it is appropriate to cause an acceleration from a dating process to a marriage-minded process. If the number one thing on your to-do list is to get real and get married, you may act with prudence, but do so in a timely fashion. Remember the appropriate timing is three dates within ten days. This means you get one week and two weekends to get something going. If the relationship isn't going to work, you will know sooner rather than later. If it is going to work, you've just caused an acceleration, speeding yourself toward your goal. You need to figure out if this is the right person for you in a reasonable amount of time. Three Dates in Ten Days will bring about an acceleration or an end. Either way it's a win!

What happens when you are dating long-distance? Yes, that again. I recently had a client who started dating someone long-distance via phone and video chat. My client told me they weren't going to meet in person until after one month of talking. She was feeling confident that the phone and Skype was helping them maintain a good velocity and progressing the relationship nicely. While I agree with her that she was maintaining a good velocity, she was doing so at the expense of never having seen him in person. This is a huge problem. If you have never met the person you're talking to, you could be advancing something which may go nowhere upon a first meeting. If possible, it is important to meet within the first two weeks of talking, especially if you think there is a connection. However, time and schedules don't always permit meeting so early. Use velocity wisely, and be careful not to let it drive you on an emotional roller coaster.

Newton's Third Law of Motion

"For every action, there is an equal and opposite reaction."

Aleeza's Third Law of Dating E-Motion

For every action, there is an equal and opposite reaction.

If you apply an e-motional force on the person you are dating, the person you are dating applies the same force on you. You are in control of the pace. Whether you choose to continue to date or to end the relationship makes no difference. What matters is that by taking action there will be a reaction, which means progress. This way the relationship will resolve, by moving forward or ending, in a timely fashion.

For those of you thinking, *"Science is not my thing. Can I have plain English please?"* – the short, sweet version is this: once you have some dating e-motion, you will tend to stay in motion. One date is not motion; it's one date. Two dates is a nice start, but you're barely out of the gate. Three Dates in Ten Days gets a relationship in motion. When in motion you will either recognize the e-motion that you are feeling or lack of e-motion and be able to decide whether or not the person you are with is right for you.

Chapter 27: Technology and Etiquette

Even in my secular days, I knew that watching TV had a negative effect on me. I knew that it was good to monitor what I watched, as well as how long. So when I became observant, the concept of not watching TV was not so foreign to me. If you want to learn more about why some observant Jews don't watch TV, just ask Rabbi Google.

When dating, my husband and I had the TV discussion. We both agreed that we did not want to own a TV. I was so happy that we were on the same page. A decade ago, owning a TV or not owning a TV was a big deal. These days you can forget about a traditional TV; we can get TV on our phones now! Not to mention our laptops, iPads... by the time this goes to print there will probably be new and improved media access. So now, even though my husband and I don't own a television, we have encountered a new dilemma. A cell phone isn't a simple cell phone; it is an invasion of the world. TV, news and social media potentially right there in your bedroom day and night. How do we create etiquette to deal with technology when it has become interwoven with our daily lives?

Imagine you're on a date, and the person you're sitting across from keeps glancing down at the iPhone that has been sitting in their lap all evening. What are they doing? Are they looking at the time, counting the minutes *until* the date is over? Are they checking email? Responding to texts?

AHH! So frustrating, I know! If I could get their attention, I would tell them to pay attention and put the phone down. What's wrong in this scene? What's wrong is that those of us on the phone instead of in the moment grew up in an age without etiquette. It makes no difference whether or not you and your date are compatible, common courtesy should be just that: common. In the olden days, about ten years ago, when people went on dates, they actually had conversations with the person sitting across from them. According to a recent study, nowadays most of us can't go 10 minutes without compulsively checking our phones. Technology has taken us out of the moment and into the world. It's time to check out of the world and check into your date.

Here's my message for those of you so attached to your phones that you can't bear to part from them for two hours: you have forgotten how to make someone else feel important. Or perhaps you were never taught. I believe you know how to make the person with you feel important. Do you give them your full attention? Do you show them that there is no one more important to you right now? Do you give each date your all, or are you eagerly awaiting the moment you can run to the bathroom so you can text your friend a status update?

Please join me for a moment of visual silence. Take your eyes off that piece of technology so you can actually focus on what is in front of you. If you do, you will be more likely to properly evaluate the date at hand. If you think that texting and driving is dangerous, forget about texting and dating. Choosing the wrong spouse is more than disappointing: it's frustrating and detrimental to your well-being. Do you want to live a life on the phone or in the moment with your spouse? This is the time to decide. And if you need to know the time, don't check the phone. That's what watches are for. Invest in one. It doesn't even have to be a Rolex. You may be thinking, *"Come on, Aleeza, get with the times."* Let me assure you, I am with the times. I own a droid, and I text. My favorite texts are the ones from my husband, the *"thinking of you and loving you"* messages. However, when dating – or married – texting etiquette is essential.

Where are your eyes focused: the next text or recognizing your future spouse? I know that I need sustained eye contact from my husband. I develop trust and love just from looking into his eyes. Remember the old line, "eyes are the windows to the soul?" Think about it.

You have my permission to use technology. Just use it wisely. Wisely in the case of technology doesn't mean using common sense, it means using etiquette.

"Fine," you say, "I'll put the phone away during dates. But there's nothing wrong with texting between dates, right?" Nuh-uh. Texting between dates is like texting at a red light: still illegal. Let's get real for a minute.

You go on a date and everything is great. Let's imagine the guy doesn't call the next day. However, he does text:

You don't respond; what else are you supposed to say?

Still not a conversation starter. Do you reply?

No reply for six hours, so you resend your message.

Or how about the following scenario: you go on a date, and it was fair. Then it just sort of ends without any confirmation of future plans. About an hour after thedate ends, she texts you:

You don't know if you want to see her again, so you don't know what to say. You wait until you think of something, but that never happens, so 24 hours later you text back:

Both of these conversations were totally unnecessary. If you are working with someone – a friend, a matchmaker or a go-between – they may be able to resolve many of your dating misunderstandings. (If you aren't, maybe now is the time to reconsider and find someone you trust to help you!) However, by not texting at all, you can avoid many of these misunderstandings. Skip texting between dates; it can be more trouble than it's worth.

What about texting to simply confirm a time or location or to let someone know you are running late? I can live with that! It is better to call, yes; but texting is acceptable in this case. Just be careful not to get too chatty and turn it into a conversation because that will not bring you success in dating. Texting to make plans is OK, but not for a schmooze.

Chapter 28: Hot Button: Breaking Down Responsibility

One of my male clients once said to me, "Dating is like a second job, except I'm paying!" Yes, yes, yes! Dating takes a tremendous amount of resources, both emotional and monetary. This is equally true for men and women.

However, I believe that there is a particular breakdown of responsibility for men and women that best leads to a successful outcome. This may be the most controversial topic in this book. But controversial is not the same as unhelpful. Read it, think about it and decide how much you will or won't incorporate these ideas into your dating life. It may not be a popular concept nowadays, but if popular hasn't worked for you yet then try reading this with an open mind.

For Men (Mostly)

Whoever coined the expression 'man up!' really got it right. Right now, I'm talking about paying for the date. The world today is drastically different than it was in the '50s. Back then it wasn't just expected that the man would pay for the date, it was assumed. There wasn't any other way. Times have changed. Today, women often earn more than the men they date. And even if they aren't earning more, they are earning enough that they can afford to pay their way... and sometimes yours. But just because she can pay doesn't mean she should. You get my drift? Just because she can doesn't make it the right way.

Now, social norms have put a lot of pressure on women. You may find that women not only want to pay but will get upset if you don't let them at least split the bill. So let's get real for a moment. What if you hold your ground? You take a woman out and you pay (at least for the first few dates). What happens? You just treated her like a lady, and you acted like a gentleman. You were the man, which in turn allowed her to be the woman. Paying for the date is an indicator of seriousness, a way of showing her that you're not just dating for the fun of it. It also demonstrates your willingness and ability to be a provider. I know in the future you may split the bills or both work to support your family. Maybe she'll work to support both of you. Any and all of that is OK. But for now, you are courting your wife. If you would like your lady to act like one, please treat her like one. She is not your buddy; she is possibly your future wife. Start your marriage out right by owning up to being the man. Keep in mind: if she is so upset that you won't let her pay that it becomes a major issue, do you really want her as a wife? A woman who doesn't know how to receive from another may be self-sufficient. While this is a good trait in some instances, it may not be a great trait in a marriage partner. Both halves in a relationship will benefit from giving and receiving. In the beginning you pay, while allowing her to give in some other way.

If you noticed, what I said above was that the man should pay for at least the first few dates. Sometimes after a few dates the woman feels very strongly about planning and paying. Since one develops love by giving, this can be her way of deepening the relationship. So if, after a few dates, she is adamant about wanting to plan and pay for a date, you can let her do so. But don't start splitting the bill. Let her pay once and then man up and go back to paying.

If you're now thinking, *"It's just too expensive to date!"* you may be right. If you think dating is expensive, wait until you have a family! Get used to money flowing out, and it will be one less thing that will frustrate you when you're married. This is no joke. If money is a real issue, get creative. Not all dates have to involve a meal or an expensive activity. Sometimes expensive dates happen when the person planning them is too lazy to think of something else. Creative dates can be inexpensive, but they will cost more in time.

There is another benefit to this model. How does one develop love? By giving. By giving your time to planning the dates and your money to paying for the dates, you will start the process of growing closer to your future wife.

What if you are thinking, *"Well, I'm not sure if this is my wife, so I don't care if she pays."* I don't think I really have to tell you that this is the wrong way to think. Simply, it's not a marriage-minded approach. If she isn't your wife, then why are you going out? If you are 100% sure, you shouldn't be wasting your time or hers. But, to quote a clients' mentor, "When in doubt, go out."

If you need to date to figure out whether or not she's the one, you can still be a mensch (person of integrity). So even if this isn't your wife, you should still pay for the date. YES, pay for the date. Why? Because you will be working on developing good character traits. Your wife, whoever she is, will appreciate that you went through the dating process and came out a better person. What's the other option? You could just keep going along, doing what you've been doing. You could be satisfied with being mediocre. But a mediocre man will usually find a mediocre wife. And I don't think that's what you're looking for.

For Women (Mostly)

Women of the world: you are far more accomplished than any generation before. You have more rights and freedoms, and more earning potential, than ever before. But use your time and efforts wisely. Please let the men *man up*. Let them plan the date and foot the bill. You want to be treated like a lady, right? You don't have to be a girly girl to want a man to be able to take care of you. You want to know he is able to support you financially as well as emotionally, physically and spiritually. Let him start by paying. It is through his actions that he will connect to you. Letting him pay for a date is an investment in your future husband's love for you.

You also have to pay. But you pay in gratitude, not in dollars. A genuine thank you goes further than splitting the bill. Below are a few suggestions for different ways to express your gratitude. Feel free to add to them if you enjoyed the date. However, leave out the embellishments if you don't plan to see him again!

Verbalizing your gratitude:

> *Gratitude and I want another date:* "Thanks so much, I had a really great time!"
>
> *Gratitude and I don't want another date:* "Thanks so much, it was so nice to meet you."
>
> *First date:* "Thank you so much for picking me up and taking me out."
>
> *Validating his choice:* "You picked out such a great place!"
>
> *Acknowledging his effort:* "Thanks for making the plans for tonight."
>
> *Noting his attention to detail:* "My favorite ice cream... you remembered! Thank you."

Other ways to express gratitude:

> *Give a token:* You know he likes chicken salad; pack some for a picnic date.
>
> *Send a note after the date.* But do it via email, don't just send a text.
>
> *Make him something.* You like baking cookies? He probably likes eating them. You know what they say: the way to a man's heart is through his stomach.

If you still have a need to pay and this chapter hasn't jarred you out of your old way of thinking, please allow him to pay for the first few dates. And while you're doing that, try this: after every date, put the amount you wanted to spend on that date into a special savings account to be fully handed over to your husband when you get married. Depending on how often you date and how generous you are, this could be quite a sum, and it will be your gift to him with no strings attached. Does the idea of handing over all your hard-earned money to your future husband in one lump sum make your skin crawl? Really? Why is it easier to give to a stranger who may not be your husband than to give to your husband? This is a lesson in giving. You are going to be married soon. You are a bride-to-be. Your husband is going to appreciate that you have practiced letting the man be the man. He will appreciate the fact that you practiced being a receiver. He will also appreciate that you are a giver and you have been giving to him after every date in preparation for your reunification. I know this idea might sound crazy. But try going on a few first dates where you let the man pay while you put $5 to $45 into an account for your future husband and see if your mind starts to shift. You might have an ah-ha! moment.

What if you don't have the desire to pay for a date and you are totally content to let him pay? You would still benefit from putting away a specific sum after each date (perhaps $15) in preparation for your future husband.

Maybe you still haven't bought into the idea of letting him pay. Consider the following. We women are already spending plenty on dates. We are paying our way in clothing and cosmetics, not to mention the myriad other treatments we pay for to take care of our appearance. It's just that we pay for those things before the date rather than on it. Yes, men groom in preparation for dates too, but not like women.

This chapter is not intended to make you feel entitled to being taken out, or to make you feel taken advantage of if he doesn't offer to pay or asks to split the bill. My goal here is for you to learn your part and for the man to learn his.

Wrap-Up for Ladies and Gents

Everyone has a role to play. Think of it like a theatrical production where each player receives his or her script. When all the actors follow the script, the play comes off beautifully. But if one actor decides, "Nah, I don't feel like wearing the costume and saying those lines...I could do better. I'll just say it my way," that one actor can ruin the whole play. How is your play going? Have you embraced your part or are you struggling to remember your lines? Want to pay for something? Take yourself out for a cup of coffee and ponder the above.

Chapter 29: Men and Women Can't Be Friends

Remember our Jewish math? A couple is made up of two bodies but they share one soul. You will often find with male/female friendships that someone is interested. This is because we are meant to be united. Therefore, we can't just be friends. Period.

Do you want to get a cup of coffee with someone casually, just to see? Maybe you're thinking, *"If this isn't my soulmate, maybe I'll make a new friend."* No. That is not a marriage-minded approach. If you feel like making a new friend, look for a friend, not a date. Your potential soulmate is not your potential new friend. Why? Because men and women can't be friends.

Let's be clear. I'm not saying you can't get a cup of coffee with a date. I'm saying you shouldn't go out casually with someone "just to see," thinking that if you only end up with a friend it will be OK, too. Those are the kinds of dates that mentally build a lack of trust in yourself. In addition to your logical mind, you also have instincts, and instincts shouldn't be ignored any more than logic. Tap into your instincts. Use your intuition, wisdom, reasoning and logic together and only go out if your date has the potential to become a spouse. "What if" or "you never know" are not reasons to date someone for marriage. I am here to remind you that you do know yourself. In fact, you are the only one who really does. Trust yourself. Differentiate dating from making friends.

The alternative is what I call Burnout Hours. Burnout comes from all the hours of dating when you knew there wasn't potential, or when the timing or person wasn't right. If you want to get real and get married, say yes to those who are right and no to those who are wrong... including potential "friends."

Chapter 30:
Another Hot Button: Hands to Yourself = Clarity

We're not quite finished with the hot topics yet. There is no gentle way of saying this: if you want clarity in a relationship sooner rather than later, you're going to have to keep your hands to yourself.

OK, now that it's out on the table, let's discuss exactly what I mean. First, I'm speaking about physical touch within the context of dating. I think it's obvious to anyone who has ever been in a physical dating relationship that clarity is very difficult when touch is also a factor. Physical touch will cloud your vision. And that's exactly where you'll be if you engage in it: in the clouds. Do people who physically connect still get married? Of course. That doesn't make it the right way to date. Some people also marry *because* of the physical aspects of the relationship, rather than the mental, emotional and spiritual aspects. But consider this:

what good will it do for you to marry someone you are physically compatible with but who in other key ways will not bring out your best self?

There is a large body of research that shows what a powerful effect even brief physical touch, like a pat on the arm or a high five, has on us, from releasing the hormone oxytocin (which can create sensations of trust) to reducing levels of the stress hormone cortisol. If you're interested in exploring this topic more deeply, there are several worthwhile books written on it, including Gila Manolson's *The Magic Touch*.

I can hear the argument coming. "But if you don't touch, what if you marry someone who turns out not to be physically compatible with you, or even attractive to you?" Yes, that is possible. But let's be fair and look at the reverse as well. What if you marry someone who you find very physically compatible, but you also find them less mentally, emotionally and spiritually compatible? How easy is that going to be to change? Honestly, you are more likely to have success in improving the physical aspects of your relationship than the emotional ones. In addition, let's evaluate your future life. How much time is going to be spent being together physically and how much time is going to be spent being together emotionally? I know you want a perfectly balanced person who suits you emotionally and physically. I think that's what we all want. I certainly want that for you! Keep in mind that the real test of compatibility comes after you are married. Yes, at that point it is too late to walk away, but over time and with work you have the opportunity to grow both your emotional and physical connection. You will have to learn together how to increase your compatibility and connection on all planes.

We may have to agree to disagree on this point. If you agree that you will have more clarity without having to consider the physical aspects of a relationship, great! If you agree that I make a good point but you just don't think you can do it, I would still suggest you try to wait for as long as possible before engaging in any physical contact, even small gestures. Waiting a minimum of four to six weeks will help you to have some clarity. If you are still dating at that point, you will at least know that you like the inside of the person enough to continue. If you can't wrap your head around this concept and totally disagree with me, I understand. It is reasonable to not understand something you've never tried. My kids thought broccoli was gross *until* they tried it. Now they affectionately call it brocc-a-tree and eat it with joy. Personally, I bought into Hands to Yourself right away. Actually, I married the second person I dated after learning about it. I won't guarantee you that success, but I do guarantee you won't regret trying it once. You may learn something about yourself. And every step you take toward gaining clarity will help you to make good decisions when choosing a spouse.

Chapter 31: Simple Checklist After Your Date

We finally made it to the post-date schmooze! So you went out with Mr. or Ms. Almost Right. Now what? Let's take time to process the thoughts going through your head when you get home after the date. Dating can sometimes be so clear. The simple "no, not for me" dates are easy to walk away from with a clear conscience. But what happens when the scales are even? Some things you like, some things you're not sure about, some things you don't prefer but you may be able to live with. And then it starts to happen:

the head spin. Do you know that feeling? Your head is filled with so many thoughts that you can't process them all. If you can't process, you are much more likely to give up on the idea and end the relationship. It's often easier to call things off than to keep trying to process thoughts that have become overwhelming. Waiting and working through the process takes patience and effort.

So how do you make it through an unclear dating process and maintain sanity? Remember that most things become clear over time. There are times when thinking can be overwhelming because you don't need to be thinking at all! At those times, what you really need is to keep dating and gathering more information. When you have enough information gathered, it is important to think about the relationship and see if it makes sense to keep dating. This process is vital because calling things off too early may cause you to miss out on your soulmate. It's true: without proper evaluation you could potentially miss your soulmate.

The following questions are here to keep your mind focused on what is important. They may also help prevent your head from spinning, thus avoiding the "I give up, let's call it quits" feeling. While these questions are simple, the answers aren't always. Some answers may be yes and others no. But if you can answer yes to a majority of the questions below, you'll know you're on the right track, and it makes sense to keep dating.

1. Do you want to know more after every date?

2. Do you have more similarities than differences with both big and small issues?

3. Is this person liked by their family and friends?

4. Do you feel safe when you are together?

5. Have you evaluated the red or yellow flags in your relationship, and are you feeling confident to move ahead?

6. Physical: could you look at this face for the rest of your life, stare into those eyes, listen to that voice?

7. Can this person help you to grow in the areas where you are weak?

8. Do you understand where this person came from (their past)? Do you connect to where they are now, in the present moment? Are you looking to build a similar future?

9. Have you spoken about the big issues like building a family, where to live and what community to be a part of?

10. Has your mood shifted toward the positive since you've started dating, or are you struggling daily to feel good about dating this person?

If you are finding that you don't know the answer to half or more of these questions, you need more time to gather information. Keep dating. The path to clarity comes both from information and from your feelings. If you don't have enough information and your feelings aren't clear, live by the mantra that things will become clear over time. Allow yourself enough time to gain clarity. Saying no and walking away from this person is a forever no. Close the door, lock it with a key and don't look back – that's clarity. If you're not ready to do that, give yourself time to process it and be patient through the process. Patience is a virtue. If it's one which you don't currently possess, get on it!

Chapter 32: There's Nothing to Tell 'Til There's Something to Show

What do I mean by something to show? I mean an engagement ring. Yes, dating can be enjoyable. Sharing stories is oh so much fun, especially when, with the click of a button, you can make the world your audience. But there's no room for status updates when you're marriage-minded. Why does your whole world have to know?

You just came back from a great date, or a horrible date, or a neutral date. What's the first thing you do when you return home? Do you speak to a family member or to a roommate? Do you pick up the phone to call the person who set you up or to call a friend? Do you change your status on social media sites? Do you tell someone the play-by-play and then ask, "What do you think?"

Checking in with someone after your date is a great idea. But I recommend doing it with care. Here are some tips for successful check-ins.

1. **Reflect on your own for 30 minutes to 1 hour or even overnight.** As a matchmaker and singles' mentor, I am much more interested in knowing what you think than in what someone else thinks. You need time for your thoughts and emotions to settle down. Remember, "This too shall pass." If you are on a high, that energy will pass; if you are feeling low, that energy will also pass. Your thoughts and feelings will be more accurate after the dust has had time to settle. And that will give you a more accurate read on how you are really feeling and how you want to proceed. Besides, what's the rush to speak

with someone? If you are set in your feelings, they'll still be there in an hour. But if you aren't set, then in an hour you will have more accurate information.

2. **Allow your relationship to grow by keeping it in the dark.** Another reason to hold back information, not only right after a date but generally speaking, is so you can live by this new motto: there is nothing to tell 'til there's something to show. You learned about choosing your five mentors. Beyond those mentors, shhh... keep it private. Give your relationship a chance to blossom. The best way to let it blossom into an engagement and marriage is to keep it private. Chatting about your date prevents the relationship from growing to its fullest potential with good speed. Why? Because growth happens in the darkness. Do you remember your parents telling you to go to bed, that you needed rest if you wanted to grow? Well it's true. Although children's growth hormones are released during the day, the real growth happens at night while they sleep. In terms of the dating process, darkness is not physical dark but rather the quiet, peaceful, restful moments where there are fewer distractions. That's the best place for your relationship to grow: in those quiet moments without distraction.

Here's another thing to consider: why would you want to chat about someone who is not your husband or wife? In the future it could cause pain or embarrassment should your spouse be compared to someone you previously dated. Not only shouldn't you speak about the person you are dating (except to your five mentors), but you would be wise not to be very public about your relationship either.

Maybe you're thinking, "Wait, does this mean I can't introduce them to my family and friends?" The answer is both yes and no. Of course, you will introduce them to family and friends at the time you determine is appropriate. This point in time will be different for everyone. Because there are so many personal factors in this area, there is no specific recipe for success. Be aware of what the common dating practice is in your social circle. Then make a decision about when to make the introduction based on whatever you feel is right for you. Don't cave in to pressure from friends or family to bring a relationship into the bright light of public scrutiny before it is ready. Keep in mind that you are not dating for pleasure but for marriage: proceed with caution.

"But what if I can't keep it private? We've been going out for four months. People know we are dating and are talking about it." First, just because someone knows doesn't mean you have to acknowledge it. They know, you know they know; you still don't have to talk about it. What will not talking about it change? Everything! Your relationship remains private from conversation, ridicule, comments and questions. And second, if you have been dating for four months, shouldn't you be thinking and talking about engagement? If you are close to engagement, you should be considering introductions.

Sometimes dating is rough. However, Shhh... Keep it Private is one thing you can do to help smooth out your dating process and empower yourself to make good decisions. The alternative is a road lined with frustration which disempowers you. I am sure you want to avoid this road. Here's a story to illustrate what I mean. A client of mine met someone and began a long-distance relationship. When I checked in with her, all was going well. One day I saw pictures of her and this special someone on Facebook. I wrote to her and reminded her of my suggestion that "There's nothing to tell 'til there's something to show. Shhh... keep it private." She sent back a picture of her with a ring on her finger! She had put pictures of the two of them up but hadn't made the announcement yet. I wished her a mazel tov and congratulated her on keeping things private! This story had a happy ending; most Facebook stories from the world of dating end something like this: "I changed my status online only to be dumped the next day." Don't fall into that trap.

Chapter 33: House Rules

You might not be thanking me for all this advice quite yet. You might be thinking instead about all the rules, guidelines and steps – the many things I'm telling you to do and not to do. I know it's a long list. It feels like a lot to do because it is. I'm asking you to make significant changes to the way you approach the world, not just dating. It's easy to look at the advice as a whole and become frustrated with the process. If you're saying, "I don't have the time!" or "It's too much!" it wouldn't be the first time I've heard those complaints. But before you decide to toss the baby out with the bathwater, let's talk about how to break the rules. Remember playing Monopoly? Everyone had their own house rules. In my house, when we rolled snake eyes (double ones) we got $500. First there are the rules. Then there are house rules, your rules.

How do we define house rules in dating? House rules are a modification of the basic rules. They are designed for your life at this point in time. They are a temporary change to dating based on your individual situation. Which means that when the situation changes and you start to date someone new, you go back to the basic rules and make exceptions when necessary. Keep in mind that while your house rules can change, the basic rules, which are your core values, don't. It is important to know your core values and uphold them. Don't throw them away just because you can't stick to them exactly in this moment! Temporarily doing things differently than you normally would, in order to accommodate a specific situation, is acceptable and often necessary.

For example, what happens when you start to date someone, and you just can't squeeze three dates into ten days? What if you meet at the busiest time of your year? Should you forget about trying to make this new relationship work, figuring it just wasn't meant to be? No. While dating this person in this moment, you need to do what will work. Should they turn out not to be your soulmate, then the next time you will still strive for Three Dates in Ten Days because it is a dating philosophy that you value and believe in. If you find yourself breaking your values more often than following them, it's time to clarify your values and decide what you can live up to.

Part IV: How Do I Know if This is The One?

Chapter 34: Patience, Persistence and Peanuts

"How do I know if this is *the one*?" Most people want a magic answer or formula to this question. The truth is that the answer is different for everyone. The knowledge of who is the right one comes at a different time and way for each individual. However, there is some common ground we can speak about to aid you in the process of identifying your spouse. This is where patience, persistence and peanuts come in.

Patience

"I've run out of patience for the dating process. I understand how the process works, I know how to play the "game," but I just want to be at the next step already!" I know that waiting for the "right time" is not easy. Remember that patience is a virtue.

I know it may not be one which you currently possess, but it is one you can start to embrace. It is precisely when you are at the end of your rope, without patience, that you can feel confident the end is near. How do I know? You can put your trust in Jewish wisdom. In his article "It's Always Darkest Just Before the Dawn," Rabbi Eliyahu Safran shares some beautiful insights into Rosh Chodesh, the Jewish new month, which relate to this. He explains that the new month is purposely celebrated not at the bright full moon but rather at the new moon, the moon's darkest point of the month. Why is this? Because Rosh Chodesh is about our belief in renewal. At every point in our history – from slavery in Egypt to exile from our land to the darkness of the Holocaust – redemption has always followed despair. "The power of the lesson of Rosh Chodesh touches every moment of Jewish experience, promising hope when hope seems furthest away and light when the night is darkest." Remember this as you make your way through the dating process. It is usually at the point where you're ready to give up that your salvation is close at hand.

Dating can be frustrating, annoying and sometimes boring! But it can be great too. The great part of dating usually comes when you meet the right one. And everyone other than your spouse is going to be the wrong one. So unless you succeed and meet your spouse the very first time you go out, you are likely to encounter challenges along the way. This is normal, and having patience with those challenges will get you from here to chuppah. Focus on increasing your patience and embracing the process. Patience in dating is no different than patience with work, health or life. If you are a quick learner and mover and have been able to control the pace of your success, you may not have needed to develop patience to a high degree. Because of that you may now feel out of control in your love life. But the truth is you do have control of one thing: you! Get a grip! Use this time to increase your patience. You are going to need the virtue of patience in marriage with in-laws, children and relatives new and old. And what if you are a slow mover? Then have patience and give yourself time to move through this process. Don't get frustrated with your own pace. Rather, understand and embrace yourself through the process. Whether you are a quick learner, a slow mover or anywhere in between, patience is a virtue and one which you would be wise to possess.

Persistence

Persistence pays. Research shows if you are persistent, you are more likely to achieve success and reach your goals. Ask an athlete why they continue to strive even after many failures, and they'll probably tell you they have learned the lesson of persistence. If you want to be married, it doesn't matter if you have been dating for a year, or five years or twenty years: don't give up on your dream! Giving up will not bring you any closer to your chuppah.

Let's see if you are just going through the motions or if you are truly being persistent. Going through the motions means that you are dating and being marriage-minded but without your heart and soul invested. Persistence means that you are dating in the way that is appropriate for you and continually pursuing your dream of marriage. My father taught me, "Inspect what you expect." Being persistent means inspecting your actions, your motivations, and whether or not you are being authentic to who you are. How can you inspect your actions? Start by keeping track of who is helping you. Your mentors should be a source of strength who make you feel empowered and self-assured. Confirm and reconfirm that they are doing a good job in supporting you as you work toward achieving your goal. If you feel something lacking in your relationships or in their support, it may be time to replace your mentor. Next, inspect your motivations. Perhaps you want to be married because you don't want to be alone. This motivation will get you married but not necessarily keep you married to the same person for a lifetime. I hope by now you realize that marriage is a lifetime of work and joy. Meeting your soulmate is as glorious as it sounds, and also as challenging. Your greatest challenge will not be your *spouse*; he or she will actually be your greatest asset. Your greatest challenge will be living with yourself while being married to your soulmate. Living, loving, learning and growing will be your new full-time hobby. And I know you are looking forward to this challenge! Like all good things in life, with the effort comes the reward. You are about to be rewarded with the greatest gift on earth. How have you prepared yourself to exert energy in this new area? Just as you have persisted in dating for months or years, you will also have to be persistent to remain married. Being marriage-minded means you will persist in both finding the right one as well as in learning how to best take care of your spouse and yourself for a lifetime.

Peanuts

Do you feel like you're working for peanuts? Men, you put time into planning dates and paying for them, and it never works out. Not only are you working for peanuts, you're paying for the experience! Women, you spend an hour or two getting ready before each date and for what? Another letdown. When you're interested, he isn't. When he's interested, you aren't. And when you're both mutually interested... oh yeah, that hasn't happened yet, or you wouldn't be reading this! You know you're working for a great payout: marriage. But when? And to whom? Isn't it enough already?!

Working for peanuts can make your dating experiences feel meaningless. Here's something to keep you going when the going gets tough. There is meaning and purpose to your dating life. All that the One Above does is for the good. Dating is one chapter in the book of your life. So how are you to understand this painful time where you work so hard for what feels like nothing?

We can't. We simply can't understand. If you were able to see your past, present and future in one glimpse, you would probably be at ease, knowing that good things were coming your way even while you were struggling. But you can't. Have you ever seen the back of a needlepoint? It looks like a mess of knots, colors and frayed ends. Seeing that wouldn't intuitively lead you to think that there was something beautiful around the corner. But turn that needlepoint over, and you see a colorful, neatly-arranged design. So too, our lives can seem messy beyond repair. But when we look at our lives from a different angle, there is usually a beautiful design. Remember to have patience and persistence when striving to reach your dream because that dream is just around the corner and you'll be thankful you made the effort. The truth is that you aren't working for peanuts. You are working towards one of the greatest goals, challenges and pleasures in life. So have patience in the process, know that persistence pays and don't work for peanuts. Instead, understand that your hard work is leading to your soulmate no matter how tangled that journey may seem.

Chapter 35: Marathon Dating vs. Decisive Dating

Here's another way to think about who is right for you. Have you ever heard the expression, "Take one step forward, two steps back"? Can you relate to that in dating? Have you ever jumped into a relationship only to realize a little later that you took action too quickly, and now you find yourself even further back than where you started? Taking a leap ahead is a great thing to do... that is, after you've first assessed yourself!

Let's talk about two opposite styles of dating: marathon dating and decisive dating. Marathon dating is when you feel that your relationship is going on and on without end. You may be exerting energy running from date to date, sweating profusely on the journey, feel the need for others to cheer you on and yet still lack the ability to know the "right" thing to do. Date after date after date doesn't seem to be getting you closer to deciding the question: *do I like you enough to marry you?* When marathon dating goes on long enough you may even consider taking a break to figure things out. While I do agree that you need to figure things out, I believe that changing styles from marathon dating to decisive dating is the best way to gain the clarity you so desire.

Decisive dating is the concept that no matter how fast or slow a relationship progresses, you will grow the relationship fastest not by taking one step forward and two steps back, but rather by first taking one step back and then taking two steps forward. What does that mean, and how do you do it? You assess yourself first. Take a step back while still in the relationship. Make sure you are clear about who you are, what you want and what direction you desire to head in. I know, I know: you already know these things. Well, yes and no. You may already know yourself well, but you don't know yourself well enough yet in relation to the new person you are dating. With some people you are quiet while others bring out your boisterous side; some make you comfortable while you are actually quite uncomfortable around others. You are you in all of these relationships, but you perform differently in each situation. Notice what sides of you this person brings out. Do you like this side of yourself? Do they bring out the best in you? Before deciding if you like them, or wasting time wondering if they like you, try deciding if you like you when you are with them. Once you've taken that step back and decided that you see your best self when you two are together, then you can take two steps forward and confidently move your relationship ahead.

Decisive Dating for the Marriage-Minded

Decisive dating means more than just making a decision about the dating process. It is also knowing that you have the ability to make decisions, big or small, that are good for you. Choosing your spouse is not exactly like picking out your shampoo; however, there is merit to knowing that you can make both large and small decisions in your life. Here's a simple one: you choose what you eat each day. And what you wear. You also choose who you associate with, how often, where and when. It's obvious that you already have the ability to be decisive. You might have also decided where to go to college, what to major in or what job to accept. If you have made any of those larger life decisions, you may feel more confident in choosing a spouse. But what if someone else made those large decisions for you? Maybe you liked the fact that you didn't have to choose. You may even be afraid to make larger life decisions, that's perfectly normal. (If you feel that fear is holding you back, I recommend

Feel the Fear... and Do It Anyway by Susan Jeffers.) However, when it comes to marriage you will be the best one qualified to give the final yes or no. Remembering that you make decisions on a daily basis will help you understand that you can make this decision too.

Making a decision can be difficult because of confusion about what is real vs. what is in your heart, mind or imagination. Fireworks and sparks, butterflies and jitters; is it real, or just a crush? This may sound counterintuitive, but if you are feeling fireworks and sparks that actually puts me on high alert. "CODE RED," my matchmaker alarm shouts. "Emergency evaluation, call in the troops!" Why? Because fireworks are dangerous, both the Fourth of July kind and the dating kind. Fireworks can lead to awesome explosions of color, sizzle and excitement. But they can just as easily lead to an explosion that leaves you missing pieces of yourself. In dating terms, a crush = infatuation. Infatuation sometimes happens in a relationship, but not always. If infatuation is absent, don't despair. You still may be dating your soulmate. If there is pleasant conversation but no spark, you may keep going out because everything keeps working and there is no reason to stop. Yet there is no reason to say yes either. The reality is that for some people there may be no defining moment where you proclaim "This is my husband!" or "This is my wife!" That defining moment may be sealed at the actual marriage ceremony. Not what fairy tales portray, I know, and perhaps not what you want to hear. Imagine how wonderful it would be if a loud voice from above said, "THIS IS THE ONE." But then we would lose our free will. And what are we here for if not to use our free will to become who we need to be? Choosing the right one is an important part of the process of actualizing your best self.

But if infatuation is present you need to be clear on what purpose it serves. The amazing sparks you feel when you are together serve to bring you closer. That lasts through engagement and hopefully into the first month or so of marriage. Once you are married, its purpose, bringing a couple together, has been fulfilled. After walking you down the aisle, infatuation leaves you to lure another couple to happily ever after.

So how can you pick the right one if you can't trust infatuation? There is an old story about a person watching a silversmith demonstrate his craft. The silver began as a dark rock. Then it was melted under fire until all the impurities burned away. The person asked the silversmith, "How do you know when the silver is ready?" "Simple," he replied. "The silver is pure when I see my own reflection in it." How do you know when you have found the right person and are ready to marry your soulmate? When you see your reflection in him or her. If you know who you are and what you look like inside and out, when you meet your soulmate you will recognize him or her. You're not meant to be carbon copies; rather your inner souls will mirror each other. Opposites may attract, but they don't always make the best marriage partners.

What if you are confused and unsure whether this is the right person? I suggest you look at them long enough to see your reflection. Allow yourself enough time to make a proper decision. But what if after the amount of time that you feel is appropriate you still aren't seeing your reflection in the potential soulmate across from you? There are several possibilities. First, do you know who you are and what you look like on the inside enough to recognize that reflection? Yes? Good. Then the reason you are struggling could simply be that the person you're staring at doesn't reflect you. In which case you aren't a match. Survey says: not your soulmate! It's OK to move on. Don't be afraid to be decisive. But if you still can't make up your mind, the next chapter is for you!

Chapter 36: Neutral Dating

Ever heard of the Law of Neutral Dating? No? That's because I invented it.

Have you been out with a really nice guy or girl, but just weren't feeling a connection? Have your friends ever told you to move on when you were feeling frustrated and undecided? I know how hard it is to try to make a decision after only one date. It's especially difficult when the man or woman seems great, but there's no spark, no special feeling. Let's talk about a few tools to help you make a choice with confidence and clarity, no matter who you're dating.

First, let's define lack of excitement. Let's call it neutral. You're not feeling butterflies, but you're not turned-off either. They're kind of nice, but are they really worth your time and effort? Let's put it in perspective: a first date is just a first date. The first question to answer: *am I repulsed by them?* If the answer is yes, that's a deal-breaker and there's nothing left to discuss. A deal-breaker is a deal-breaker: if there is something that you can't get over right now, then this doesn't work for you. There shouldn't be any judgment attached to your choice. You need to make your decision based on who you are right now. Later you can work on who you want to be for the future.

Am I repulsed by them? If the answer is no, if you aren't turned-off by them and yet you don't like them either, then you don't have enough information. Not having butterflies is just one little piece of the puzzle. It's not enough to call it off.

Here is the Law of Neutral Dating: if you're feeling neutral, you continue dating until the answer becomes clear to you. Then you'll be either in drive or park. Drive means moving forward. Park means never looking at this match again: you have fully investigated and you have clarity that there is something that does not work. Park is kaput, finished, done, no thank you.

If you aren't in park but also aren't clearly in drive, sometimes instinct says, "I know myself, and since I don't feel it, I've gotta move on." Resist the impulse to end things too quickly and give yourself the opportunity to get to know the other person. It's possible that you can never find nice guys or girls because you never give yourself the opportunity to get to know them. I mean really know them. Try to enjoy the process and be present in it while on the date. Even if you aren't excited about another date, if you do decide to go out, don't hold back. After all, at this point you have nothing to lose. Ask everything you're curious about; explore anything that doesn't feel right. Fully investigate this person so that if you walk away you can do it with confidence. You should be able to smile at the end and say, "I made the right decision."

People often ask, "Isn't that lying, or leading them on?" The answer is: NO. You're not lying to them or to yourself. It's normal to be unsure. If you aren't sure then gathering information is the right thing. Besides, if you were attracted to someone on the outside but unsure whether you liked the inside, would another date be lying to yourself and them? Would you call it off? Probably not. Why? Because you would want to see if the inside matched up with the outside. Infatuation can keep you going longer than necessary. But when the tables are turned and you love the inside but not what your eyes see, often you can't find the patience to let your eyes catch up to your brain. And it's important to give yourself that time to catch up. How much time? About three to seven dates.

I recently followed up with a man who struggled with his eyes during the dating process. In the process of dating his future wife, Michael* loved the inside but was neutral about the outside. Actually, to be fair, his future wife was not the thinnest gal. She was average plus, and he was trying to be neutral about her looks. Through the dating process he got support to help him figure out if he could look at her for the rest of his life. Not only look at her, but build a strong, loving, caring relationship and not wake up feeling disappointed daily. In my follow-up call several months after he was married I asked, "So are her looks still an issue for you?" He chuckled as he told me, "Not at all." He was excited to tell me they were expecting their first child and didn't take my question too seriously. And he's not the only one. Several other clients I followed up with who had expressed similar concerns now gave me similar answers.

Here's another story. Sara* went out with Dave* we spoke when she came back from their first date. She had heard amazing things about him, and before they even met, she was convinced he was the one. But after the first date, she was not just neutral but neutral minus. Everything he had said was negative. He was negative about a family vacation, about work... you get the picture. When I asked her, "What was positive? What did you like about him?" there was silence on the other end of the line. A few seconds went by and she couldn't come up with a single thing. Even if someone doesn't have what you want or need, you can still see good things in them. Everyone has good traits. I knew if she couldn't find one positive thing, she wasn't really present in the moment of the date but living in her thoughts. I suggested she go out again without expectations. I told her that sometimes you need to change how you see, not what you see. The things you don't like are very obvious, and sometimes you're so focused on them that you miss all the things you do like. After seeing both sides clearly it is easier to make a decision and weigh your options carefully. My conversation with Sara was very different after her second date. She raved about Dave and how generous, kind, considerate and thoughtful he was. It turned out that he had had an awful trip and was going through a rough time at work, and he had felt comfortable enough with her to share it all with her on the first date. (This is a good time to mention that there is a time and place for sharing personal information. Although you may be feeling close enough to share private information, a first date is not the ideal time to put all your cards on the table. If you want to reach a second date, it is in your best interest to keep personal and private information for a time when you are both feeling close.)

Sometimes the person in front of you is amazing. If you aren't looking at them in a way that allows you to see them clearly you may miss them all together. Giving yourself more time to adjust your view can have dramatic results. However, three or four dates should be long enough to clear your vision. If after four dates you're still stuck in neutral, and you aren't more interested or curious, I would recommend looking within to see what's really bothering you. There is probably something else going on that you haven't considered, a deal-breaker you aren't fully aware of yet. (If you're someone who struggles with anxiety or fear you may need five to eight dates to make this decision.) You have gut instincts that will clue you in to what you need to know, but you may not always have the information to back up the instinct. Most often you're right, but on occasion you're wrong, and that's why gathering enough information is important. Allow yourself enough time to get more information so you can see and evaluate your potential spouse clearly. Most things become clear over time.

Now, if you can't bring yourself to say yes to that second date, if you feel strongly, then that's not neutral. You're in park, you just haven't figured out why yet. Remember, it is possible that he's a nice guy or she's a nice girl and he or she is still not for you.

Chapter 37: For the Ladies: Size and Cycle

Right now you and I are going to take a big leap and leave the world of dating. At some point on your journey you will be making a change in status from dating to engaged. Although you may not have that person in your life at this moment, you will soon. The following chapters discuss a few things you will want to keep in mind as you approach the transition to engagement.

Size

Don't get excited, I'm not speaking about the size of the rock! What I actually want to know, ladies, is this: do you know your ring size? Particularly the size for the ring finger of your left hand? Now, it's not mandatory to have a ring the right size from the get-go, but it is a nice perk. I knew a girl who had to put two Band-Aids around her engagement ring because her finger was a size 3 and the ring was a size 7! And it's even more frustrating when the ring fits your pinky and there's no way you can wear it. If you know your ring size you can either drop hints or send the message via a friend so he can get it right and save you both the frustration. An alternative utilized by some Jewish couples is getting engaged with a different piece of jewelry, usually a bracelet. The ring comes later, allowing the couple time to pick out a ring together.

Whether with a ring or a bracelet, it's time to enjoy! The dating and engagement process is stressful enough. When engagement arrives, it's time to put some effort into relaxing and remembering to have fun with the details. You are making memories for a lifetime. You are now writing the opening lines to the story of your marriage. Make it sweet!

Cycle

I'm speaking about your monthly cycle. Men: You can read or skip, but it's helpful information for you to know as well. Women: Start charting your menstrual cycle. You are going to be planning a wedding soon, and you will need to know the ideal times to get married so you don't end up mid-cycle on your big day. Having a history of at least six months would be helpful in predicting the future. If you've been charting for a while now, pat yourself on the back and keep it up! If not, or if you have no idea what I'm talking about, get a book on cycle or talk to one of your mentors. Basically, you need to know the first day of your cycle and the last day of your cycle, and you should mark whether it began in the evening or daytime. That information compiled over the course of several months should be enough to work out an optimal wedding date.

Chapter 38: For the Men: EmpoweRING

I have a feeling that, based on the title, the women are going to be much more excited about this chapter than the men. How do we empower ourselves during the engagement process? Let's begin with some basics. One of the basics of engagement is an engagement ring. Interestingly, the giving of a ring is not a Jewish custom. Really, there is no Jewish custom to give a ring at engagement. Actually, the opposite is true: it is customary not to give a ring at engagement. In the Jewish tradition, we use a ring under the chuppah. (There is much more to say on this topic so if you are curious, please ask your local rabbi.)

Although an engagement ring is not a traditional Jewish custom, it has become a common practice in some (not all) circles of Judaism. Others, as I said before, may be giving a bracelet instead. But either way, men: if you are serious about being engaged and married this year, you would be wise to start a jewelry fund. For those of you who are already ahead of me, way to go! For those of you thinking, "Huh? I thought I was reading this book to find the right one not get advice about saving money and buying jewelry..." go start your fund. You're going to find her. And when you do, you're going to want to give her something, right? So, what do you need to do to make that happen? First, open a savings account. Put $350 in your jewelry account today. If you can put $1,000 to 2,000 away, that would be better. You're going to need money to buy two rings. One ring is for your wedding; it will be a simple band without any adornments that you will give your bride under the chuppah. The other piece of jewelry is what people traditionally refer to as an engagement ring (or bracelet). How much do you need to put away into the jewelry fund? That depends on who you are and who your wife is! I have heard many different formulas. Some say two months' salary. But if you aren't working for whatever reason, double nothing is still nothing. But that's OK. Brainstorm a little bit and make a plan that works for you. And remember, the ring is not the important part; the marriage is!

A Ring in the Family

What if you have a ring in the family? Great! You just saved yourself a chunk of change. Now here's where things might get tricky. What if that ring is from a divorce? Does it have bad karma? Great question.

If you have a diamond ring that is in the family but was from a divorce, I have good news: a diamond is a diamond, is a diamond, is a diamond. Diamonds are bought and sold all the time. If you think yours is fresh out of the mine, think again. I'm not just sharing information: I bought a diamond from a divorcee.

Let me tell you my wedding ring story. I didn't receive a traditional ring when I got engaged. My husband was between jobs, and at the time I wasn't "into" rings. Actually, I was one of those girls who secretly wanted a ring but thought it was too materialistic. I told my intended not to buy me a ring and instead to see if there was anything in the family that could be passed down. His mother lovingly gave him three rings to choose from. Two of the rings, one a diamond and the other a ruby, were traditional engagement settings. The third ring was unique. My husband had difficulty describing it because its form was more like a bracelet than a ring and didn't have the classic stone. He asked me the day before we got engaged if I wanted to see the rings and pick one. I told him that if he let me see a ring, I would put it on and not take it off! So I told him to pick and suggested that he choose the more unique ring as his bride would probably prefer it.

Keep in mind, men, that buying a diamond sometime in your future is most likely even if you get out of buying one for the engagement. Take the second half of my ring story. Several years after my own marriage, a woman called me saying she had a diamond ring she wanted to sell. She needed the cash and didn't want the memories. She asked if I knew anyone who was getting engaged who would maybe want to buy it. I had no one in mind at the time but said I would keep my ears open. Two weeks after that phone call I decided it was time that I received a traditional ring. Our fifth anniversary was approaching and I was finally ready to embrace the jewelry-loving side of myself. I had also just learned that women should receive either clothing or jewelry on Sukkos, Pesach and Shavuos. Our anniversary falls right after Sukkos, so it seemed like the perfect time to get a ring without feeling materialistic. I called the woman back and told her I was interested in buying her ring myself! I popped the diamond out of the old setting, put it in a new one and voila – I had a ring. Some women might cringe at the thought of a diamond from a divorce. I'm not advising you to get a ring with any particular history; I just wanted to bring up the topic in case you encounter this kind of diamond in the family.

So men, to sum up: Either save for a ring now or find out if there is one in the family you can have. You are getting real and getting married so you need to start thinking and planning. Remember to buy your wives gifts of clothing or jewelry on Sukkos, Pesach and Shavuos. And one last friendly tip: as soon as the ring is in your possession, INSURE IT!

 Conclusion

What do I want you to take away from this book? I can summarize it in one quick acronym: SELF. What is SELF? It's the basics of what this book, and my program, is about. SELF is four pillars that will bring you success in the dating process and beyond. They are: Support, Empower, Listen and Find. Let's break it down.

Support comes from having the right pieces in place. It is being in the right place for you, a place of stability. It is having the right mentors, matchmakers and go-to people. It is feeling comfortable and confident in your support system.

Empower is the knowledge that you know what you need and that you have everything you need to get it for yourself. You know who you are and who you are looking for and you have permission from yourself to go for it.

Listen is just what it sounds like, but it might just be the trickiest part. It is listening to all your little voices and instincts. It's trusting yourself. But it's also filtering out any outside information, all the noise that comes from everyone else's opinions, so you can hear yourself clearly.

And *Find* is the last step: going out into the world to find the person who is a perfect match for you. Notice that Find is the last step; Support, Empower and Listen come first. Remember, more suggestions aren't always the answer. The answers lie in you.

What are your dreams? How can you help yourself to reach your heart's greatest desires? Is being engaged a year from today (or sooner) impossible? I don't think so. I did it. Many of my clients have done it. For years people thought that it was impossible to run a mile in under four minutes. Then someone who knew it was possible came along and tried and tried until the record was finally broken. First the negative thoughts were broken, then the record. The barrier has already been broken. You can get real and get married. Now it's time to break into new habits.

You can do that by making small daily positive efforts towards your goal. It may at times seem as if you are making an enormous effort for something that you can't achieve. It might seem that way right up until you reach engagement. Remember, you will often see no results from your actions... until your engagement and wedding, that is. But you must strengthen your faith, trust in the dating-for-marriage process and know that the One Above is on your side, looking out for you. You can't see the tiny movements happening behind the scenes. You don't see things lining up so your dream can become a reality. However, know that they are happening. Dating for marriage won't bring you instant gratification. But a healthy, good marriage will bring you lasting feelings of love, joy and success!

I hope you have gained self-knowledge, dating techniques and an understanding of what you need to be doing moment-to-moment. I hope your faith and trust in dating for marriage has been restored and that you have the energy to endure the rest of the journey. May your journey be sweet, may your soulmate be close and may you have the right people in your life to assist you on your way.

With gratitude to the One Above,

Aleeza

Bonus Chapter: A Little Humor for the Road

The dating and engagement process can be exhausting. It takes searching deeply within ourselves to both be and find the right one. And in the merit of all your hard work, I am including some humor to put a smile on your face and in your heart. Humor can carry you through this time period and make it bearable. As you know, a smile on a date can make everyone feel at ease. I am sure you have your own funny dating stories and one-liners. Those stories will help you to embrace the waiting with humor. There is no time like the present to change your attitude and inner light. In order to shine you will need a twinkle in your eye, a smile on your face and humor in your heart. So sit back and enjoy a little humor from my experiences with my clients.

Client Quotables

On relationship development:
> *It's rather like watching a tree grow. Quiet and slow and profoundly boring to those not directly involved.*

On picking up signals:
> *I think this one went well! I think it was pretty obvious.*
> *(Then again add only two letters and you get oblivious.)*

On Hands to Yourself:

Celibacy is not like fine wine: it does not get better with age.

On Internet dating:

I've been trying to find an apartment on Craigslist. Half the ads are scams, the other half are psychos, and the last half don't get back to you. It's a lot like dating, actually.

On growth in the dark:

Things definitely grow in the dark. You should have seen what stuff was growing in our fridge at work. Thank G-d for hurricane Sandy and losing power for a week. They had to dump the contents of the whole fridge and get a chemical hazmat team to clean it afterwards. Oh, that's probably not the "dark" that you are talking about.

On engagement:

So we should talk. Um, I think I am engaged? I think that's what happened last night? Yeah, that's basically what happened.

On practical steps:

I like your action plans, but you should call them: 'What to do while your mother prays for a miracle.'

After meeting dad:

I like him. He's normal for a change.

Conversationally Speaking

Client: *Can I date someone who just returned from overseas?*

Aleeza: Dating jetlagged girls is like dating drunk men.
Not appropriate!

Client: *I am a dog person, and I just don't want to give up my pet, but the girl I'm dating is allergic.*

Aleeza: You'll enjoy sleeping next to the wife more than the dog. Fish are nice though, and hypo-allergenic. And seriously, if you are more attached to the animal than to the human, do you really want to get married? They do talk back!

Client: *You sure there isn't another name in your little black book?*

Aleeza: I've got tons of names in my black book. But you already have her name on your heart so there is no room for another unless she is not in your life. I'm a tough cookie, but you don't pay me to be polite. You said you want to be married. I believe you. Let's make it happen. Date her and see if there is something there, or let go and let's find your wife. Out with the old, in with the new. I know you would prefer to have dinner with the old and look for the new at the same time, but that isn't a marriage-minded approach. Dating is OK if that's what you want to do. But you don't need me to help you find a date. I look for wives, not dates.

Client: *Priceless.*

To follow Aleeza's blog, get up-to-date

information on upcoming events and other exciting news,

or to book her for an event,

visit

www.MarriageMindedMentor.com

www.twitter.com/aleezabenshalom

www.facebook.com/getrealgetmarried